Transformational Leadership

A Framework to End Poverty

How to tap into your community's wisdom to end poverty and thrive

Dismantle the poverty management system and lead your community through the four stages of transformational change

SCOTT C. MILLER

Copyright 2019

Transformational Leadership

By Scott C. Miller, Founder of Circles USA

SECTION 1: TRANSFORMATIONAL LEADERSHIP	7
Changing the Mindset—Can We Believe in Ending Poverty?	7
Introducing Culture Change	8
A Deeper Look into Poverty in U.S. Culture	9
Reducing Poverty Rates	10
Bootstraps and Benefits	11
A Tipping Point to Begin the End of Poverty	13
Leadership to Solve a Wicked Problem like Poverty	14
Introduction to the Transformational Map and Matrix	17
The Transformational Map Matrix	19
Reflections	21
SECTION 2: VISION	22
Why Vision is Important	22
Individual Change Precedes Social Change	22
Being the Change is Essential to Leading Transformation	24
The Hero's Journey	25
Letting Go of Delay Patterns	27
Heart-Centered Leadership	28
A Case for Change and a Preferred Future	29
Organizational Mission Statements	30
Understanding and Choosing High-Impact Strategies	30
Evaluating Strategies	30
Content to Inform Your Strategies	34
A Tipping Point	34
Transformational Leadership	34
Shifting from Poverty Management to Poverty Reduction	34
Collaborating with Diverse Experts	35
Transactional Programs to Relational Programs	35

Cliff Effect Mitigation	36
Community Allies	36
Relevant Education	36
Cross-Sector Partnerships for Job Creation	36
Research, Data, and Accountability	37
Increasing Poverty IQ	37
Communicating Your Vision	**38**
Are You a Visionary, Facilitator, or Practitioner?	39
High-Impact Communication Strategy	41
Leading Versus Managing	42
Scott Miller's Example of Preferred Future	43
Questions for Reflection	46
SECTION 3: ALIGNING WITH OTHERS	**51**
The Top Management Team(s)	52
Practices and Procedures	53
Archetypal Roles in Organizations	54
Building a Shared Vision	56
Criteria for a Transformational Plan	57
Self-Reflection Questions	59
People Hear the Call to Adventure Differently	**60**
Four Common Responses to Poverty	61
Why the Call to Adventure in the United States is Complicated	67
The Call to the Business and Education Sectors	71
The Call to the Human Service, Government, Civic, and Philanthropic Sectors	74
Linking the Poverty Reduction System to a Job Creation System	75
Undergirding the Poverty Reduction System with a Relational Strategy	76
Building an Intentional Community to Reduce Poverty	77
Building a Productive and Appreciative Culture	78
Poverty Reduction System Teams	79
The Call to Adventure from Circles USA	80
Tips for Aligning One's Own Job and Life to the Vision	**81**
What is Your Story?	81
Aligning the Environment	84

Aligning Everything Else	85
Self-Reflection Questions	86
SECTION 4: FACILITATING LEARNING	87
Self-Reflection Questions	88
Refining your Personal Learning Agenda	89
Self-Reflection Questions	90
Other People's Learning Agendas	91
Facilitating the Learning Curves	91
The New Metrics of our Vision	92
SECTION 5: EMBEDDING CHANGE	94
Mental Model for Ending Poverty	95
What are the New Structures of Sustainability?	96
Unchanging Values	97
Self-Reflection Questions	98
Supporting the Next Generation of Leaders	99
Self-Reflection Questions	99
Be the Change: Center of the Map	100
Completing our Transformational Journey	101

SECTION 1: TRANSFORMATIONAL LEADERSHIP

Welcome to the Transformational Leadership Program for Poverty Reduction Labs. This program guide provides you and your Leadership Team with tools and reflections for leading a transformation. Certainly, anyone who is sincere about finding solutions must embrace the moral commitment to end poverty rather than just "manage" it. While many will disagree with making a commitment to end poverty for fear of appearing naïve, most will agree to the idea of doing whatever is possible to reduce it by at least 10% in hopes that such a tipping point might accelerate the process.

Changing the Mindset—Can We Believe in Ending Poverty?

One person can make a difference, and everyone should try.
— *John F. Kennedy*

I was in New York City a few years ago having a conversation with a former United Nations ambassador about my first book, *Until It's Gone, Ending Poverty in our Nation, in our Lifetime*. He asked me several questions about my assumptions regarding the nature of poverty and about my work at Circles USA. After 30 minutes of dialogue, he revealed what was really behind his questioning when he said to me, "Jesus said the poor will always be with us. Is ending poverty going against the Bible?"

The former ambassador was not alone in asking this question. For many in the nation, the biblical proclamation that "the poor will always be with us" strongly suggests that no matter what we do, we will always have poverty. From this point of view, any attempt to eradicate poverty is a task that has no hope of success. Perhaps the best that we can hope for is to manage poverty or maybe save a few people. But can we believe in ending poverty? Yes, I believe we can do it, but only if we change our mind-set.

Through the Transformational Leadership Program, we will review assumptions about high-impact strategies that are worth investing time and resources in pursuing. *High impact* means the effort aims to change the mind-set that created the organization or system of organizations. The mind-set informs the goals that shape the programs of the organization. To create a system to end poverty requires that the system change its entire culture.

For example, when people don't believe that the poverty rate can be reduced, let alone eliminated, they create a poverty management system. To change that system, we will have to apply resources toward affecting the deeper beliefs that shape the system's culture. How can we can challenge such a dominating belief be challenged?

I took the former ambassador's belief that "the poor will always be with us" to a theologian who works closely with a Circles USA chapter and discovered that the original teaching has been taken out of context. If one Googles "the poor will always be with us," she or he will find evidence of this confusion with warnings not to use this statement to discourage social action. Additionally, many passages in the Bible suggest a much more active stance toward the poor.

While this example from Christianity is a useful teaching tool, Circles USA partners with a range of secular and religious organizations. Circles USA's inclusive, nonpartisan community welcomes people from all faiths, ethnic backgrounds, sexual orientations, and socioeconomic classes. Understanding the beliefs of these diverse community stakeholders is key.

Introducing Culture Change

Culture eats strategy for breakfast.[1] It's an illustrative phrase to warn executives that you cannot change the strategy of a community, an organization, or a system, without focusing on culture and the beliefs people hold about how things work.

At Circles USA, we've changed the culture of poverty by tapping the power of a culture of prosperity. Whenever people have an experience that contradicts a negative reality that they have been normalizing, healing occurs. For example, participants in poverty are called Circles Leaders, and they lead the process to achieve their own economic stability. Because typically those in poverty have been dismissed and marginalized, a powerful healing occurs through the acknowledgement that Circles Leaders are the poverty experts and must be at the planning table to find real solutions on behalf of the entire community.

The idea of a poverty reduction system powerfully contradicts executives who are immersed in the management of requirements for a fragmented and random array of community programs. They feel genuine excitement about focusing on how to rearrange work into clearer pathways that actually lead people out of poverty and reduce poverty rates.

As more coherence emerges in the human services sector, we can find opportunities to enlist other sectors in ending poverty. For example, in workforce development, employers can challenge their mind-sets about employees with backgrounds in poverty and implement responsive ways to do business in order to be more successful.

---

[1] The phrase "Culture eats strategy for breakfast" has been attributed to business guru Peter Drucker although some question whether he said it at all.

Teachers can integrate pedagogies for engaging children from homes in poverty. Civic groups can question their hidden biases and rules that make it difficult for those in poverty to feel welcomed. Philanthropic organizations can analyze whether their funding practices favor short-term wins at the exclusion of long-term gains. Whatever the challenges, Transformational Leaders engage in crucial conversations that generate a cohesive shared vision of ending poverty.

A Deeper Look into Poverty in U.S. Culture

The European roots of the United States come from nations whose cultures permitted and even encouraged a significant disparity between a small ruling class and the masses, in which poverty was typical. Severing political connections to Great Britain, the founders of the United States in the 1776 Declaration of Independence aspired to equality although the systems they created replicated many old patterns. European settlers viewed indigenous people as necessary to convert and control. The Industrial Revolution of the mid-1800s followed patterns established by military organizations originally meant to serve the interests of kings and queens. The captains of industry exercised authoritarian rule over laborers and amassed fortunes in the process. Schools developed to serve the agricultural economy as well as new industrial enterprises, especially those that utilized the assembly line technology. Today, these systems still resemble early efforts to create a conforming labor pool.

While the Declaration of Independence claimed that everyone has the right to "life, liberty, and the pursuit of happiness," the United States has not made the political changes necessary to fully realize this vision. For example, slavery was not abolished until 1865. Black males achieved the right to vote only in 1870, women the right to vote in 1920, and it took until 1964 to ban segregation in public places and employment discrimination based on race. At present, the United States has one of the world's highest rates of incarceration. The culture of racism continues to negatively influence who can move out of poverty. White males have approximately a 300-year head start in getting ahead financially. To use a baseball metaphor, if one starts on third base, did he actually hit that triple and deserve all the entitlement associated with the feat?

The American Dream suggests that hard work will lead to social mobility. With the mantra "bigger is better," business leaders have argued against putting any limit on what people might earn due to fear that it will stunt economic growth domestically and push entrepreneurs to move their companies abroad. Meanwhile, the world's population has grown approximately 10 times in the past three centuries. Having 7 billion people share the Earth challenges the idea of unlimited growth: How can we sustain our biosystems while we continue to reward unlimited growth and the consumption of our natural resources?

The economy that first existed in the United States did not produce a middle class. The growth of a middle class came from the Homestead Act of 1862 and the Morrill Land-Grant Act of 1862, which made land available for farms and schools; from the creation of the Federal Deposit Insurance Corporation made banking secure for citizens in 1933;

from the establishment of the Federal Housing Administration in 1934, which made home buying financially safe; from the labor policies of the mid-1930s and the Social Security Act of 1935, which provided an array of new benefits and protections to workers; from the 1944 GI Bill, which gave grants to millions of veterans to attend college; and from the Pell Grants of 1965, which made it possible for even more people to attend college.

Growing up in the 1960s and 1970s, I directly benefited from these policies that produced a strong middle class. In recent decades, however, there have been no major policies that have reduced poverty nor increased the size of the middle class. In fact, many policymakers have become concerned about a middle class that is shrinking. To reduce poverty rates, Transformational Leaders can advocate for policies that educate and empower lower- and middle-income groups to create wealth and pursue sustainable careers in the emerging economy.

Reducing Poverty Rates

President Lyndon B. Johnson introduced War on Poverty legislation in 1964, which created programs that became our modern-day social safety net. In 1963-64, a Social Security administrator named Mollie Orshansky devised a poverty rate based on a formula using the cost of a subsistence food budget. Income roughly three times the cost of that food budget was considered to put families above the poverty line. Those official poverty rates have remained an important longitudinal barometer.

However, unequal inflation rates for necessities such as healthcare and housing have caused census analysts to create updated calculations known as the Supplemental Poverty Measure and Alternative Poverty Measure. Using these more accurate calculations, researchers at Columbia University calculated new poverty rates from 1967 to 2012 and compared them to the official poverty rates. While the official poverty rate was stable at 12% to 15%, the updated measures showed that the poverty rate was 25.6% prior to 1967 and has dropped to 16% today.

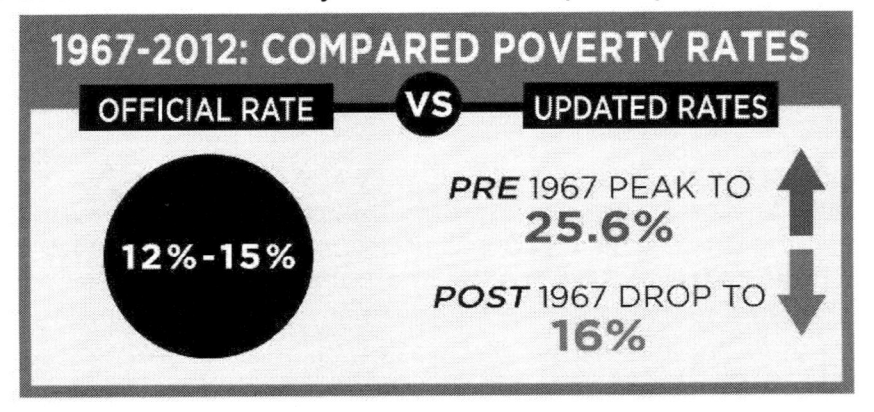

1967-2012: COMPARED POVERTY RATES

OFFICIAL RATE — VS — UPDATED RATES

12%-15%

PRE 1967 PEAK TO 25.6%

POST 1967 DROP TO 16%

Furthermore, researchers compared the updated poverty measures for a five-year time period (2007-2012) with and without government safety-net programs such as benefits provided by the U.S. Department of Housing and Urban Development (HUD); the Special Supplemental Nutrition Program for Women, Infants, and Children (WIC); Temporary Assistance for Needy Families (TANF); and others. Without government programs, poverty rates would have increased 5.1%, but with those programs, poverty rates rose only 1.3%.[2] The updated measures are more accurate and reveal how important government programs are in managing poverty rates.

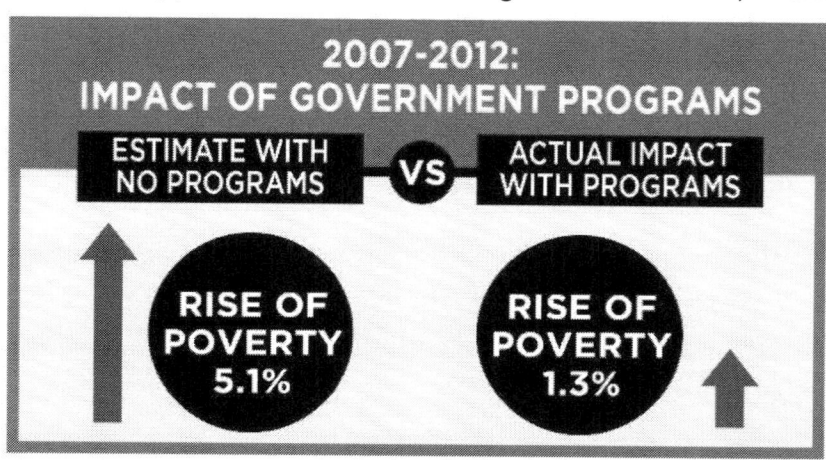

To inspire a communitywide intention to reduce poverty, Circles USA emphasizes getting children out of poverty as a focus of necessary system changes. Instead of saying, "Let's get all the children out of poverty right away," we recommend the goal of assisting 10% of children (along with their families) out of poverty as a starting place in order to provoke a tipping point that over time could more quickly help the other 90% escape poverty as well. Additionally, it's easier for people to withhold judgment about poverty when focused on the innocence of children. The next two sections include more about ideology and tipping points.

Bootstraps and Benefits

Ideology, more often than not, drives policy. Denise Rhoades, a fervent conservative and Circles USA enthusiast, approached me after hearing my panel remarks at the Fall 2015 Midwestern Governors Association conference on poverty and commented, "You are a progressive with a conservative accent." Bemused, I asked her what she meant. She said that my focus on economic development, job creation, qualifying people for the workforce, and changing the accountability of the system are topics on which both progressives and conservatives can agree.

---

[2] For more detailed information, please see the 2016 report by the Office of Human Services Policy, Office of the Assistant Secretary for Planning and Evaluation, U.S. Department of Health and Human Services, "Poverty in the United States: 50-Year Trends and Safety Net Impacts."
https://aspe.hhs.gov/system/files/pdf/154286/50YearTrends.pdf

Denise and I continued our conversation, and she suggested that we write a book together, which we did, titled *Bootstraps and Benefits: What the Right and Left Understand about Poverty and How We Can Work Together for Lasting Solutions*. In it, we describe ideological assumptions of those who believe in creating more benefit programs and those who believe in offering bootstrap incentives. Generalizing about benefit programs and a "bootstrap" approach is fraught with opportunities for misunderstanding and fault finding. Yet, for those who would appreciate more explanation of what we mean by Bootstraps and Benefits, here are a few broad-stroke generalizations:

BENEFITS	BOOTSTRAPS
Favors expanded role and growth of government rather than a shrinking government	Favors limited role and growth of government over an expansion of government
Asks what society can do to improve the circumstances of groups of people	Asks what individuals can do to improve their own circumstances
Assumes that humanity is hardwired for good. Trouble comes from sources outside of people and must be overcome collectively.	Assumes that humanity is hardwired for misbehavior. Trouble comes from within and must be overcome individually.
Assumes that, as citizens, we want to help	Assumes that, as citizens, we want to be left alone
Except when we don't.	We seriously want to be left alone.

Our book appreciates both perspectives, while keeping a focus on reducing the poverty rate by 10% and supporting families to achieve 200% of the federal poverty level (FPL). The FPL for a family of four is roughly $25,000, so we aim for a family of this size to earn twice that income or roughly $50,000 annually.

Focusing on clear goals is a unifying way to address the differences between conservative and liberal political ideologies. It isn't necessary to agree or compromise on key values when we are disciplined in working together to achieve mutual goals. We can avoid arguing about hot topics by viewing them as distractions that prevent us from supporting people out of poverty.

With regard to legislation, administrations will always support policies consistent with their party's viewpoints. Thus, our work must align with both right and left policy opportunities that show efficacy in reducing poverty rates. Furthermore, evidence shows that poverty rates go down when the economy is producing more and better jobs. Therefore, Transformational Leaders should become interested in economic development planning in order to align poverty reduction efforts with the emerging economy.

A Tipping Point to Begin the End of Poverty

During more than 20 years of speaking to communities throughout the United States and Canada, I have been making the statement that we can end poverty and should do so. I have never encountered any resistance to the idea that we should end poverty. It's the way we can end poverty that causes people to object with statements such as, "We have been fighting the War on Poverty over 50 years, and it's only gotten worse." But have we really been fighting all these years? I would say no; we haven't had a national goal to eliminate poverty.

First, the war in Vietnam increasingly distracted the Johnson administration's focus away from the War on Poverty. Some safety net programs were implemented, such as the Food Stamp Act of 1964 and the Social Security Act of 1965 that created Medicare and Medicaid. However, these safety nets created an array of allopathic remedies. Some would argue these remedies make people too busy with paperwork to get their basic needs met and lessen the urgency of finding a job. This is a poverty management system.

Furthermore, there are no financial incentives from federal agencies to support people as they move out of poverty and increase their stability. The baby boomers provided such a substantial labor pool that local economies did not need to worry about qualifying those in poverty for the workforce. Without pressure from business to demand more qualified workers, poverty management continues in government and with human services organizations addressing basic needs and elements of workforce readiness rather than coordinating all the developmental stages of transitioning from poverty into sustainable jobs.

Our strong belief is that human beings can eradicate the condition of poverty. The challenge is not whether we have enough resources to do it—because we have enough. It is not whether we know how to make the necessary systemic changes—because we know enough. Rather, the challenge is aligning the conviction that we can and should end it. Because society could be easily overwhelmed by the massive task of ending poverty in the face of realities described above, we need a smaller, yet powerful, initial goal.

Based on his network science research, Boleslaw Szymanski, Professor at the Rensselaer Polytechnic Institute states, "When the number of committed opinion holders is below 10%, there is no visible progress in the spread of ideas. It would literally take the amount of time comparable to the age of the universe for this size group to reach the majority. Once that number grows above 10%, the idea spreads like flame."

We have all seen in our time social movements such as the ban of smoking in public spaces and stricter drunk driving laws and prevention campaigns that reached a tipping point and fundamentally changed society. How can we intentionally lead in a manner that causes a tipping point in our society? Achieving a tipping point is the goal Circles USA is using to inspire and equip leaders to build Poverty Reduction Labs and Circles chapters to support 10% of households in their communities to climb out of poverty. The theoretical potential of a tipping point is that once that 10% is reached, momentum will take over, and the process of reducing poverty will become easier as more people embrace the effort.

Meeting resistance from within our own minds, as well as from those in our communities, we will need to align our intention to be Transformational Leaders. We need to follow our conviction about ending poverty, no matter what we confront along the way. Otherwise, we will likely return to the status quo and collude with a poverty management system that maintains poverty.

The guiding principle for this Transformational Leadership Program is to "become the change you want to see happen."[3] If you assert the belief that we can support 10% of children out of poverty, you will eventually find others who want to join you. Together, you can build toward a tipping point of people who will mobilize a new poverty reduction system around that goal in your community.

We are each hardwired to want to make a difference in the world. This book provides an easy-to-follow process for examining your own beliefs about ending poverty and leading your community through a transformation toward ending poverty in our lifetime. This process includes applying evidence-based models and methods from the field of Continuous Quality Improvement (CQI).

Leadership to Solve a Wicked Problem like Poverty

Researchers Rittel and Webber suggest that most public policy problems are "wicked"—that is, "[t]hey are inherently resistant to a clear definition and an agreed solution." Tackling wicked problems requires attention to complexity, uncertainty, and disagreement.

---

[3] "Be the change that you wish to see in the world" has been attributed to Mahatma Gandhi although Wikiquote attributes the principle to Arleen Lorrance at the Teleos Institute.

In their article "Wicked Problems: Implications for Public Policy and Management," authors Brian W. Head and John Alford are cautiously optimistic about solving such problems.[4]

Articles by Horst W. J. Rittel and Melvin M. Webber speak to three styles of leadership in solving wicked problems. These categories have continued to evolve over the past several decades:

> The first example is a corporate hero, where the leader maps out a vision for everyone, provides diagnosis of the problem, and indicates which strategies to pursue. In this style of leadership, the leader prescribes solutions and applies their leadership to gain compliance from others.
>
> The second style is adaptive leadership, in which the leader focuses on the engagement and mobilization of their team around problem solving.
>
> The third example is collaborative leadership, a model in which people equitably shared power. Leaders come together to ". . . frame the issues, orchestrate the agenda, recognize particular expertise, engage in win-win negotiations, spot entrepreneurial opportunities, and generally engage in diplomacy."

While Rittel and Webber use the term *Transformational Leadership* interchangeably with *corporate hero*, our definition of Transformational Leadership combines all three styles because effective leadership is dependent on a leader being able to adapt her or his approach to the demands of context, complexity, and urgency.

You will need to tap into your core values as an initiator in pursuit of the vision of ending poverty in your community. You will need to articulate the persistence to end poverty as a non-negotiable value to others in order to recruit like-minded leaders, as well as followers, to join the cause. But it will take a collaborative team of leaders to ensure that a shared vision for reducing poverty is communicated to and taken up by all sectors of the community. This team, collectively, will need to create and facilitate an environment that fosters learning and innovation. Finally, the team will need to embed transformation of the poverty reduction system into long-lasting policy, programs, and funding, all while supporting the next generation of leaders.

Of course, we're not suggesting that you attempt to force people to do things your way. We encourage you to be inclusive in encouraging others to lead, generating their own diagnosis of the problem, and suggesting possible solutions to be tested. You need to produce a process of collective will to solve the wicked problem of poverty. This requires using the wisdom of power versus force. With self-awareness, power is derived from your clarity regarding what you want to change. Force is manipulating others to follow your will. As Rittel and Webber said, ". . . [I]n the absence of clear and definitive solutions . . . you don't so much 'solve' a wicked problem as you help stakeholders

---

[4] B. W. Head and J. Alford (2015). Wicked Problems: Implications for Public Policy and Management, Administration & Society, 47(6), pp. 711-739, doi:10.1177/0095399713481601.

negotiate shared understanding and shared meaning about the problem and its possible solutions. The objective of the work is coherent action, not final solution."

Crucial to your leadership capacity is your personal coherence about your non-negotiable values, your self-awareness about what drives your desire to see a change in the world, and your clarity about the Transformational Map. Given the mission to end poverty, lives are at stake, time is of the essence, and there is a particular and essential contribution that only each of us can personally fulfill. If we accept the call, many people's lives are potentially changed for the better. And most certainly, our own life will be transformed. The emotional reward inherent in the Hero's Journey is a deeply satisfying experience for everyone who answers the call to adventure.

We each hear the call to adventure differently. It might seem like a random series of events that leads us to a crossroads where we must decide which social cause to pursue. In this book, we dissuade you from dabbling in many different opportunities; such indecision is what Campbell refers to as "refusing the call." Taking a journey that is rich in both risks and rewards requires a commitment to go long and deeply into a specific path.

Introduction to the Transformational Map and Matrix

Leading societal change can be an overwhelming proposition. It's like crossing the ocean for the first time. We all want navigational tools to know where we are and how to make course corrections to reach our destination. The Transformational Map was developed by Circles USA (formerly known as Move the Mountain Leadership Center) during a 12-year period with funding from the Annie E. Casey Foundation. The Transformational Map was tested with leaders of nonprofit organizations and community action agencies that have a federal mandate to end poverty. We provided leadership development training and coaching to help leaders shift the attention of their agencies from managing poverty with low-impact strategies to reducing poverty with high-impact strategies. Drawn from this experience and beyond, this Transformational Leadership Program takes you through a straightforward process of ensuring that your time and talents are channeled into a purposeful direction.

All transformational efforts go through a cycle of four stages:

1. Articulating the vision.
2. Aligning with relevant Allies, including people and organizations.
3. Learning whatever is necessary in pursuit of the vision.
4. Embedding the vision into the culture.

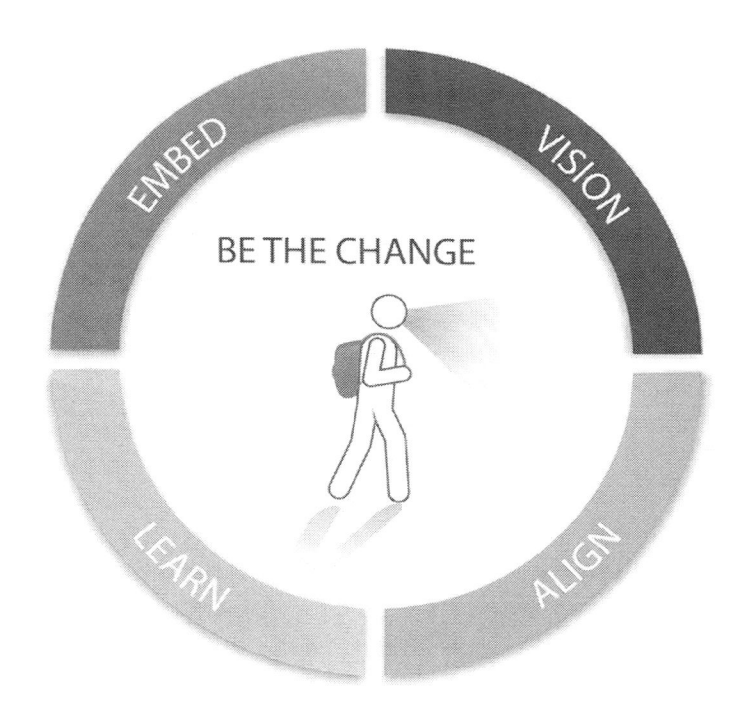

Our vision must be clear in order to avoid confusion when communicating it to others. We need to be able to articulate it in one minute, in a Ted Talk format, and in longer public speaking opportunities. It needs to be repeated with consistency by our leadership team. The vision must be compelling, urgent, and feel like something that we can accomplish. We must also identify the high-impact strategies that will allow us to achieve the vision.

Once we have a clear and compelling vision, we can begin the process of aligning with others to achieve the vision. Who in the other sectors of our society are already moving in this direction? How can we join them? Which organizations have the most capacity? Which can we build effective partnerships with, and is this the right time to proceed?

What has to be learned in order to achieve the vision? How will we facilitate this learning agenda? What metrics will we use to know whether we are making progress and when we should make course corrections? How will our personal learning affect our ability to lead change?

How do we embed the transformational changes into the culture? What programs, policies, and cultural changes must occur for the change to be lasting? Who are the next generation of leaders, and how will we support them to take our place?

By using the Transformational Map as a primary reference tool, this program will help you identify and clarify what you need to do in each of the four stages of the change process: visioning, aligning, learning, and embedding. The plan that you develop will emerge from a strategic analysis of the people and organizations you need to align with to achieve a more powerful shared vision. For lasting and positive change, you will also detail what you and others must learn in order to embed your transformation into the community.

Understanding the stages of the Transformational Map helps leaders to achieve individual and social change. For example, when feeling stuck, whether when things are not changing fast enough or in the way you desire, you can look at the map for guidance and next steps: "Am I stuck in any particular stage? Have I forgotten to mindfully and continuously engage in the cycle? What steps can I take to advance to the next stage?"

The Transformational Map Matrix

The Transformational Map matrix can be used to help you diagnose issues along the way. The matrix shows the symptoms experienced by team members when a component needs to be shored up. For example, a lack of clear vision, mission, strategies, and desired outcomes can produce confusion. A lack of shared vision can produce very slow change. Without a strong plan, there will be false starts and other obstacles. You can use the matrix to quickly see which action to take when negativity arises.

Because leaders are often keyed into the emotions of others, this chart is popular with those we work with in poverty reduction labs. If you can identify the feelings that people are experiencing, you can often point out the problem to others and work on solutions. People are quicker to relax and focus on forward progress once they understand the cause of their distress.

VISION	ALIGNMENT			LEARN		EMBED		RED FLAGS	
✓ Vision, Mission, Strategies, Outcomes *The "why & what"*	✓ Shared Vision *The "who"*	✓ Establish Plan *The "who, what, when, where and how"*	✓ Secure Resources *More "how"*	✓ Train and support *More "how"*	✓ Measure results and evaluate *Revisit the "what"*	✓ Establish new policies and programs *More "how"*	✓ Grow next generation of Leader *More "how"*	= Ø	SUCCESSFUL TRANSFORMATION
Ø	✓	✓	✓	✓	✓	✓	✓	Confusion	Clarity
✓	Ø	✓	✓	✓	✓	✓	✓	Slow Change	Consistent Momentum
✓	✓	Ø	✓	✓	✓	✓	✓	False Starts	Solid Foundations
✓	✓	✓	Ø	✓	✓	✓	✓	Overwork/ Frustration	Balanced Workload
✓	✓	✓	✓	Ø	✓	✓	✓	Anxiety	Confidence
✓	✓	✓	✓	✓	Ø	✓	✓	Ennui	Purposefulness
✓	✓	✓	✓	✓	✓	Ø	✓	Unsustained	Sustained Growth
✓	✓	✓	✓	✓	✓	✓	Ø	Unsustained	Sustained Growth

Reflections

1. Do you believe we can end poverty?
   Please note your numerical response.

NO				MAYBE					YES
1	2	3	4	5	6	7	8	9	10

2. What dominant beliefs about poverty did you hear growing up?

3. What dominant beliefs about poverty shape the culture of your community and your organization?

4. With regard to the Bootstraps and Benefits ideologies, where would you place yourself on the scale below? Where would you place your community? Where would you place your organization's board and top management team?

	Far left: The system must change	Middle left	Near left	Neutral	Near right	Middle right	Far right: The individual must change
You							
Your community							
Your organization							

SECTION 2: VISION

Why Vision is Important

Without vision, the matrix tells us that people feel confusion and a lack of motivation to change. Pain will push people so far, but then vision must pull them toward something attractive. Without vision, old habits persist, and situations will continue to deteriorate. Vision must provide a compelling case for change, a strong description of what could happen if, for example, we ended poverty. And it must provide two or three high-impact strategies that let people know that the vision can be achieved.

Individual Change Precedes Social Change

Just as in the cycles of nature, you will move through each of the four seasons of the change process. The first task is to develop a clear understanding of your own vision and purpose.

The future enters into us, in order to transform itself in us, long before it happens.
— Rainer Maria Rilke

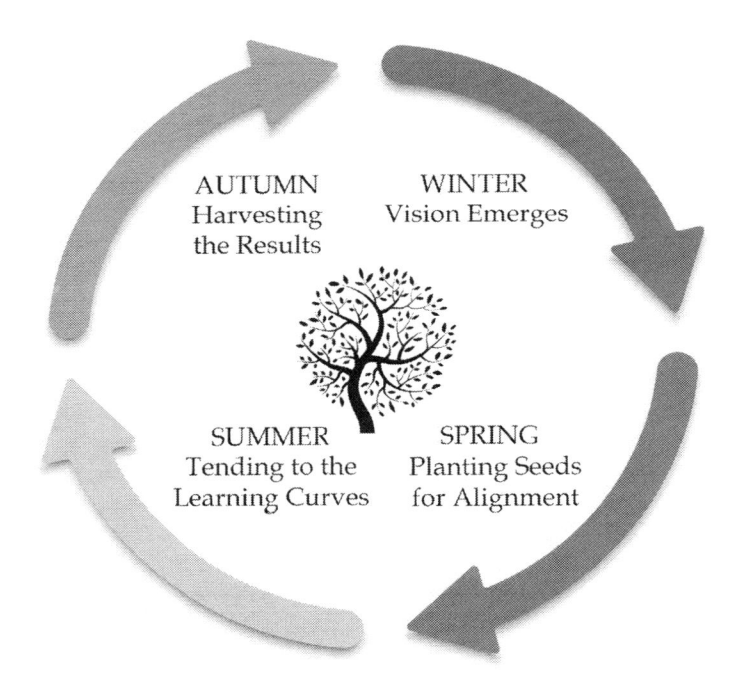

AUTUMN — Harvesting the Results
WINTER — Vision Emerges
SPRING — Planting Seeds for Alignment
SUMMER — Tending to the Learning Curves

When we wish to change something in the world, there is often something in our own lives that we want to explore, assess, and change as well. For example, in my early job experience serving people struggling in poverty, I realized how often people seemed alone with their problems. So, I created support groups as a response to such isolation. Then I looked at my own life and asked, "Where do I feel too alone in my own problems? How can I give myself more support?"

It became apparent that before I could make any lasting social change, I had to commit to changing my own life. Circles USA was the result of an intense soul-searching process that I began in the mid-1990s. Circles is a process of surrounding yourself with people who will be Allies as you make an important change, such as moving out of poverty.

A fundamental assumption underlying our approach is that each of us is more powerful than we give ourselves credit for. One might think global questions are only for world leaders to answer, but it takes only one person to send a breakthrough idea around the world at lightning speed. When we listen to our hearts, make a commitment to action, form a circle of supportive Allies, learn whatever is necessary, and embed change into the culture, the world can be positively impacted.

Through Circles USA, I have watched people change from being passive and feeling invisible to building happier, fuller lives, including the pursuit of a social change agenda on a national stage. Each of us has the wherewithal to overcome a perceived limitation and make a big difference in the world.

You have more potential than you are tapping into right now. Claim the next chapter of your life as the one in which you listen even more attentively to your heart's desire—and then act on it. You can achieve balance and become even happier than you thought possible. This happiness is both the guidance system and the engine driving your ability to influence change in the world. If you feel energized and joyful as you anticipate undertaking new plans, know that you are on the right track.

Doing good holds the power to transform us on the inside and then ripple out in ever-expanding circles that positively impact the world at large.
— Shari Arison

Being the Change is Essential to Leading Transformation

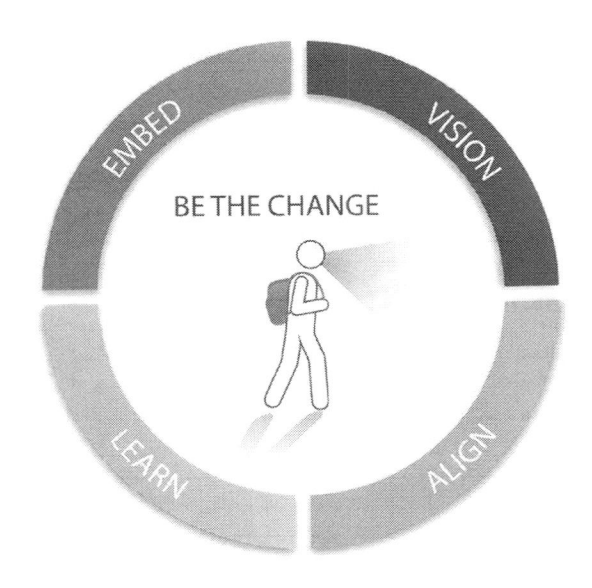

. . . transformed people transform people.

— Richard Rohr

To be the change we want to see happen is the lynchpin of the Transformational Map. Dedication to personal growth fosters positive change in the world. How can I change my life so that it's in alignment with my vision for the world? When we embrace transformation as our personal assignment, we inspire and equip others as well.

I met Diane Pike and Arleen Lorrance, directors of Teleos Institute (consciousnesswork.com), in 1979 at the impressionable age of 21, and they have been a major source of guidance and motivation for my personal growth and development ever since. Diane and Arleen met in 1971 and have been teaching their practical and profound principles through books, workshops, retreats, and speeches ever since.

Diane is the widow of Bishop James A. Pike, who, during a time marked by antiwar and civil rights protests, was a foremost change agent. He was featured on the cover of *Time* magazine in November 1966. On a trip to Israel in 1969, researching a new book they were writing on the historical Jesus, the Pikes got lost in the Judean desert. Tragically, Bishop Pike did not survive. Diane wrote a book called *Search* about the experience and was on national TV talk shows due to her late husband's fame and her extraordinary story of survival.

Meanwhile, Arleen was teaching in New York City and was inspired to express and adopt a set of universal life principles. One of these principles was *be the change you want to see happen*. According to reliable and thorough investigations, Arleen is the original source of the immensely popular phrase, *be the change*, even though it is often attributed to Gandhi.

Diane and Arleen's Love Principles have been serving me for decades:

- *Receive all people as beautiful exactly as they are.*
- *Be the change you want to see happen, instead of trying to change anyone else.*
- *Create your own reality consciously.*
- *Provide others with opportunities to give.*
- *Have no expectations but rather abundant expectancy.*
- *Problems are opportunities.*
- *Remember, choice is the life process.*

Whether you ascribe to these or similar principles, Transformational Leaders must consciously shift from reaction to response, especially when confronted with the resistance to change that is inevitable. A deep commitment to one's convictions is essential: Why do I want to realize this particular change? What does it mean to me? What more do I need to change in myself to be consistent with my values? Such self-awareness will ground you when confronting opposition. To be the change, your personal goals and values must be in alignment with the goals and values of the change you are guiding as a transformational leader.

The Hero's Journey

At a dinner honoring author Joseph Campbell in the late 1980s, filmmaker George Lucas said, "It's possible that if I had not run across him, I would still be writing *Star Wars* today. . .. He is a really wonderful man, and he has become my Yoda."

By reviewing mythological stories from around the world and throughout history, Campbell articulated a universal story with predictable stages that all humans live by. He called it the Hero's Journey. Campbell was a brilliant scholar and teacher who also coined the famous phrase, *follow your bliss*, as a life formula for his students. Campbell's work is one way to understand the emotional landscape of the Transformational Map.

I read Campbell's book *The Hero with a Thousand Faces* in college and then came across his writings again much later in life. Having lived for 40 years in between readings, I saw new value in his insights about human stories. For decades, I traveled around the country asking people to join a movement to begin the end of poverty. Campbell's work made me appreciate that my invitation was actually "a call to adventure" and that I am encouraging people to "become a hero." What is the nature of this journey that requires and nurtures the quality of heroism? Campbell offers a predictable sequence that unfolds during any hero's journey: the element of mystery, the fear of the unknown, potential of peril, aid, guidance, reward, and the opportunity for greater peace and contentment.

Here is an adapted sequence of the Hero's Journey:

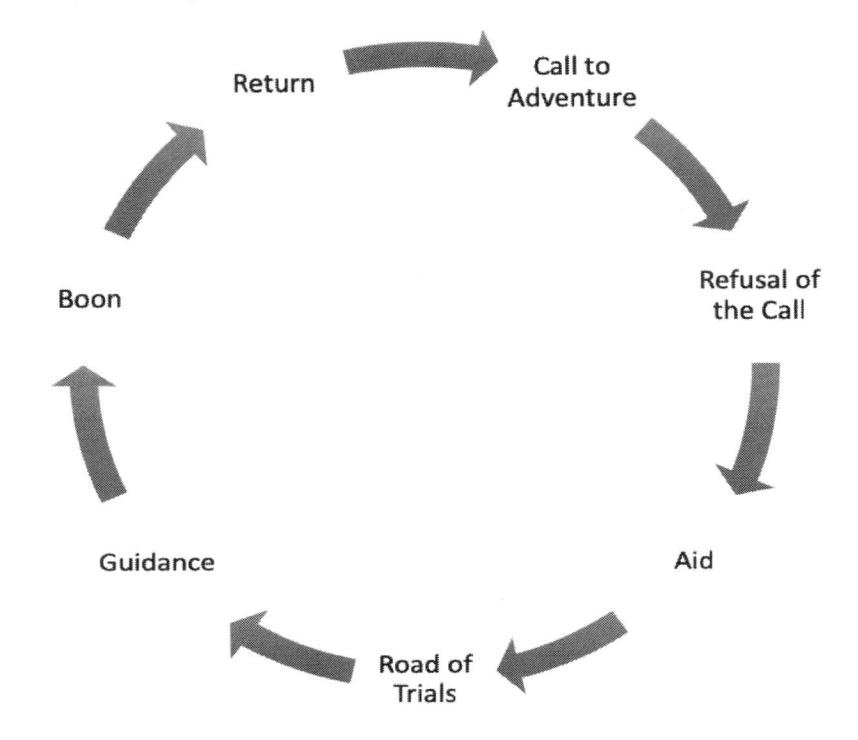

Call to Adventure → Refusal of the Call → Aid → Road of Trials → Guidance → Boon → Return → (cycle continues)

- A call to adventure starts the cycle; a hero is asked to enter the unknown to accomplish something deeply important to him- or herself and others.
- Typically, the hero initially refuses the call. However, the powerful call creates a persistent conflict.
- Aid comes from others who give the hero specific information to resolve inner conflict that the hero experiences before the adventure begins.
- When external challenges appear, the hero's conviction is deepened by confronting and overcoming each test faced over a road of trials.
- Continued guidance from others supports the hero on the journey.

- The hero perseveres and eventually is rewarded with something significant—a benefit that is both meaningful and worthwhile—and attainable only by taking the Hero's Journey.
- Finally, the return home gives the hero a new and transformed sense of self; the world is improved through the benefit achieved by the journey.

Poverty is a large, complicated, and serious problem; undertaking its solution provides anyone with all of the elements required for a true Hero's Journey.

Letting Go of Delay Patterns

While the stages of the Transformational Map might appear to be simple, each contains aspects that need to be successfully managed to complete a cycle. In this complexity, we might obstruct, disrupt, and sometimes even derail our journey. When we are able to recognize and anticipate when delay patterns are activated, we can choose more productive behaviors. Most Transformational Maps are abandoned or delayed by old and familiar patterns, rather than by taking direct action on insights and inner guidance.

One of the most common delay patterns looks like this:

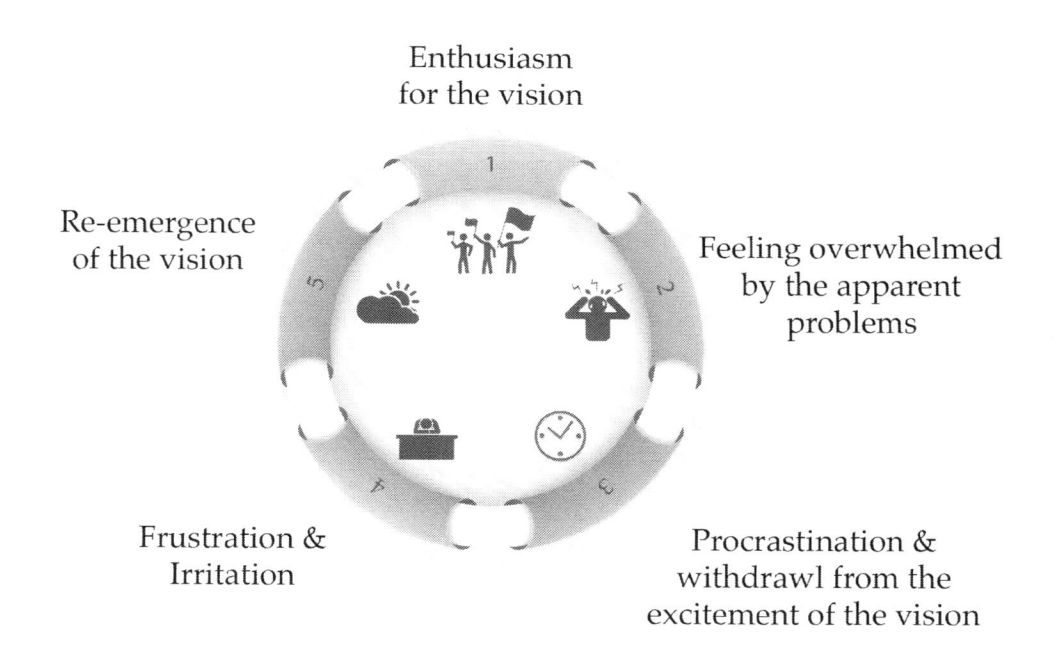

Enthusiasm for the vision

Re-emergence of the vision

Feeling overwhelmed by the apparent problems

Frustration & Irritation

Procrastination & withdrawl from the excitement of the vision

Patterns have a beginning, middle, and end; they are self-reinforcing. All patterns have a psychological payoff. For example, a pay-off is the avoidance of uncomfortable feelings that come with change. We exchange anxiety of the unknown for feelings of discouragement. Giving in to this pattern, one can eventually become discouraged, and our inner vision becomes clouded by doubt.

Patterns can be insidious, influencing life at individual, organizational, and societal levels. If we were free of such patterns, we would make decisions that are in everyone's best interests and would be able to resolve challenges with more ease. To be effective leaders, we can change ourselves by observing, interrupting, and replacing delay patterns with more productive, conscious behaviors. The commitment to becoming mindful of our possible patterns, while focusing on an important social change, is a key to moving through the Transformational Map.

Heart-Centered Leadership

In order for each of us to sustain the Transformational Leader role long enough to complete the Transformational Map's cycle, we need to articulate our non-negotiable values and a heart-felt vision for bringing them more fully into the work. In his book *The Hope: a Guide to Spiritual Activism*, Andrew Harvey challenges us to do something about the condition in the world that brings us the most pain.[5] What breaks our hearts? Asking this question can help identify our strongest values.

Once we answer this question thoroughly enough, our vision will take more substantial shape. We must feel passionate about the world we want to see happen. Others will be listening to our emotional tone, our insistence that this problem or issue must be resolved. Our "case for change" announces to people that the current reality is unacceptable and that a new "preferred future" is possible and necessary. Having listened to our own instincts about what must change, we are ready to articulate it in such a way that we can repeat it as often as needed to align others to our vision.

---

[5] Andrew Harvey. *The Hope: A Guide to Spiritual Activism.*

A Case for Change and a Preferred Future

Your vision for ending poverty needs to be spoken and written in your words. A vision includes
- A case for why we need a new system to end poverty, including both pain of the unjust present and the promise of a preferred future. This becomes your personal leadership mission statement to use as you better align with your own organization and others in your community.
- Two or three tangible strategies that your potential stakeholders can believe will work. This statement should be brief, but as interest and time from the listener(s) permit, you can offer more detail.
- A call to action that asks the listener(s) to join you in achieving the vision.

It can help to hear examples from others. Here's **my case for ending poverty with a preferred future**: What if it were possible to eradicate poverty? Imagine what that would be like:
- No longer would children go hungry; no longer would parents be wracked with anxiety about how to pay for healthcare and medicine, utilities, gas in the car, and rent.
- No longer would those of us who have plenty be disconnected from those who do not have enough.

- We would have easy pathways to provide effective support so that all are able to meet their basic needs.
- We would be invited into productive and rewarding relationships with those who seek to overcome poverty, and together we would find the path to the eradication of poverty.
- We as individuals and as a community could thrive at an unprecedented level.

See the end of this section for a sample vision narrative.

Organizational Mission Statements

You then summarize your agenda in a mission statement that briefly describes the essence of what you are doing. Circles USA's mission statement is to inspire and equip communities and families to end poverty and thrive. The statement informs all of Circles USA's activities. As a member of Circles USA, if I am not inspiring and equipping community leaders and families to end poverty, then I am off-purpose, and I feel a corresponding drain of energy. Once you have a statement that truly resonates with your leadership goals, it will provide reliable feedback about the relevance of your day-to-day activities.

Understanding and Choosing High-Impact Strategies

Strategies answer the question: What approaches can achieve transformational change? Strategies are the key major activities you employ to achieve the vision. It will be important to define current strategies and to measure their impact against your preferred future. You might modify your strategies over time, depending on how well they work. Which strategies will change the mindset of the community? Only those strategies that change mindsets will truly transform a community.

Evaluating Strategies

The following chart outlines nine leverage points for intervening in a system. As you can see, the highest impact strategies are those that change people's belief system. Once their belief system changes, they will change their goals and rules, feedback loops will change, and so on, throughout the system. But if we concentrate on simply changing the numbers (*more vouchers for emergency food*) rather than changing the belief system (*e.g., we believe that everyone should have enough food, no matter what it takes*), then the system doesn't change, and, in this example, people still do not have enough food. You will want to have a robust debate with your colleagues about which strategies are worth pursuing. You are looking for the most essential use of time and resources.

HIGH impact strategies affect

— The way people think and what they believe
— The goals of the system
— The rules of the system
— The ability of people to self-organize

MEDIUM impact strategies provide

— How information is communicated to people
— Checks and balances so that things don't get worse
— Reactions to changes in the environment rather than proactive strategies

LOW impact strategies include

— Activity that is unaccountable to the vision or mission
— Activity that maintains status quo or actually make things worse, such as enabling the community to ignore poverty by telling them, "We are taking care of it," or enabling people in poverty to stay stuck in it by providing handouts without offering self-sufficiency planning

EVALUATING STRATEGIES: Listed in order of least effective to most effective.

Impact	System leverage points	Description	Examples
Low	9. Numbers	Focuses on amounts. Doesn't really change behaviors or how things work in a community.	Focuses primarily on providing units of emergency assistance without intervening in the problem.
Low	8. Material stocks and flows	The structures we have to work with in a system.	Focuses primarily on increasing the size of the agency budget.
Low	7. Regulating negative feedback loops	Responds when our level of resources might change from stable levels (money, volunteers, staff tenure).	Focuses primarily on reacting to legislative cuts in funding of services.
Medium	6. Driving positive feedback loops	Self-reinforcing: the more it works, the more it gains power to work some more.	An individual development account program that provides matched savings.
Medium	5. Information flows	Who gets what information when.	Circulating frequent progress reports throughout the agency and community on what is working to diminish poverty.
Medium	4. Rules of the system	Boundaries, scope of the system, amount of freedom one has in the system.	Changing job descriptions and agency policies to give employees more flexibility to pursue high-impact strategies.
High	3. Power of self-organization	The ability of people to change themselves by developing their own new structures and behaviors.	Agency practice to form new teams quickly to pursue high-impact strategies. Helping citizens organize to solve their own neighborhood's problems.
High	2. Goals of the System	Where the system is organized to go.	Focuses on making the goal of welfare reform to help families completely out of poverty, not just off welfare.
High	1. The mind-set out of which the system arises	Society's deepest beliefs about how the world works.	Focuses on building effective relationships between people in poverty with those who are not so that enough people will want to do whatever it takes to help them out of poverty.

Adapted from an article by Donella Meadows, published in the winter 1997 issue of *Whole Earth*.
For full article, go to: http://www.wholeearthmag.com/ArticleBin/109.html

> Does someone want to lead the change required to make this a high-impact strategy?
>
> If so, can he or she do it?
>
> Is it important enough in our mix of strategies to invest in the leadership required to implement them?
>
> Does this activity distract our core leadership team's attention away from higher-level impact strategies?
>
> Are we engaging the community in carrying out this activity—or are we simply providing a service in isolation from the community?

The following questions can help lead your evaluation of your current strategies.

For decades, Circles USA has tested theories, refined methodologies, and built an extensive network of leaders. Here are our top high-impact **strategies**:

- Communicate a non-negotiable commitment to support families so that they have enough money to cover their basic expenses and extra money to save for the future.
- Inspire and equip communities in at least 10% of the U.S. counties to reduce the poverty rate by at least 10% and create a tipping point that can begin a nationwide movement to end poverty.
- Inspire and equip the next generation of emerging leaders to end poverty through a Transformational Leadership Program and poverty reduction design process.

Content to Inform Your Strategies

The following content areas are important to Circles USA's strategies for ending poverty.

A Tipping Point

A tipping point, such as reducing poverty rates in the United States by 10% within 10 years, could drastically reduce the number of adults and children living in poverty. Gaining widespread commitment could be a game changer.

Transformational Leadership

Leaders need a process for transformational change and a robust community of practice. They need more coaching that inspires and challenges them to function at even higher levels of performance. In order to remain urgent about transforming the community, they need enough direct contact with those they are ultimately helping through their leadership work. Leaders need to be reminded, and often need to be supported, to delegate management activities so that they can dedicate the required time necessary to truly lead.

Shifting from Poverty Management to Poverty Reduction

Our current system results in the management of poverty rather than reducing poverty rates. We are accountable only to delivering units of service in an ecosystem of poverty management programs with silos in crisis intervention, stabilization, workforce readiness, job placement, and advancement. A new and alternative poverty reduction system must more comprehensively support people through all five stages of self-sufficiency in order to drastically affect poverty rates.

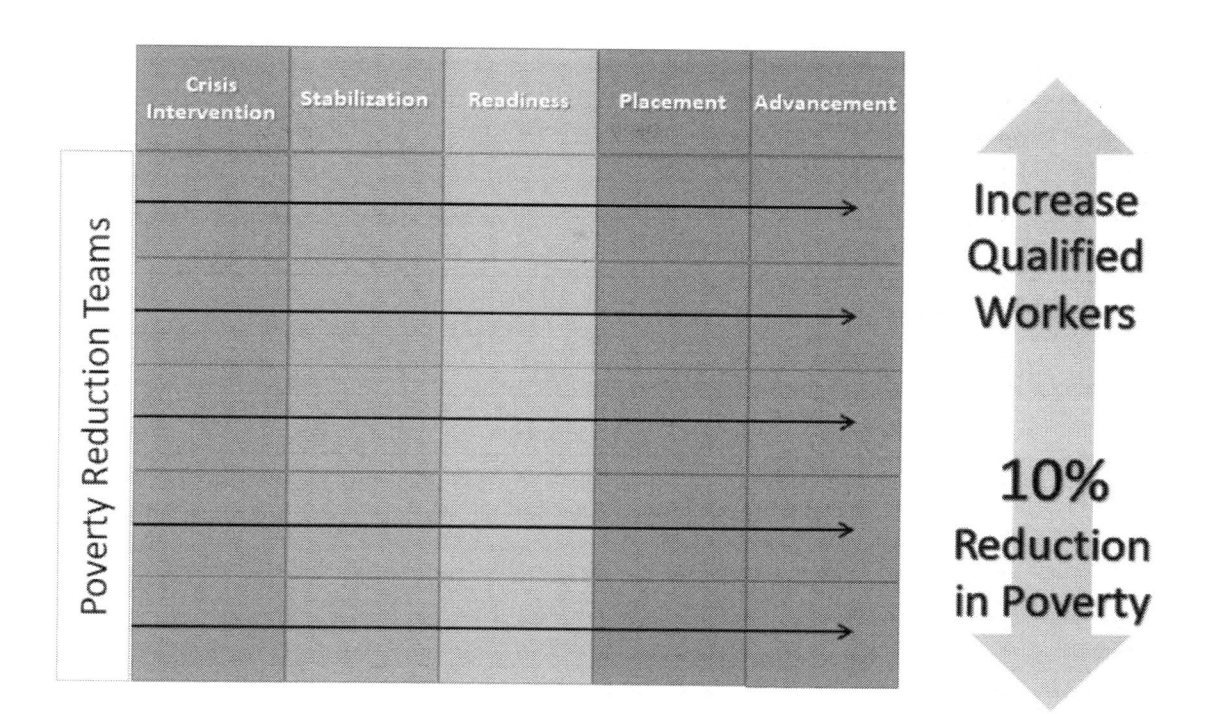

	Crisis Intervention	Stabilization	Readiness	Placement	Advancement

Poverty Reduction Teams → Increase Qualified Workers / 10% Reduction in Poverty

Collaborating with Diverse Experts

Poverty programs must be designed in collaboration with people who have successfully navigated their way out of poverty. In addition, because all six sectors of community life influence the poverty rate, we must engage leaders from business, government, education, human services, and philanthropy. Let's convene people who know how to start successful businesses, create jobs, solve messy systemic problems, reinvent organizations, redirect funding streams, and tell inspiring stories. We want those people to interact and challenge each other—and to interact and be challenged by those with direct experience of poverty.

Transactional Programs to Relational Programs

We can complement transactional programs that manage poverty with relational, community-based approaches. Circles is one example of the latter, which systematically breaks the cycle of poverty through a proven curriculum of pre-placement training, weekly support meetings, and local Allies who help to move candidates through the predictable barriers to success. These activities leverage social capital to help those effectively use existing education and workforce programs to escape poverty. Furthermore, Circles USA can be adapted for numerous groups, such as those coming out of prison, drug abuse treatment programs, domestic violence, generational poverty, situational poverty, mental health therapy, urban poverty, rural poverty, and even suburban poverty.

Cliff Effect Mitigation

To unleash the phantom workforce of those who could work but believe they can't "afford" to, we must eliminate disincentives built into safety net programs such as childcare assistance, food stamps, Medicaid, housing assistance, and Temporary Assistance for Needy Families. Circles USA is working with foundations and other leaders in several states to expose the problems caused by cliff effects and to initiate policy solutions.

Community Allies

We can call for an unprecedented number of community volunteers to partner with families who are committed to getting out of poverty and becoming economically stable. At Circles USA, we are partnering with national associations to recruit and train such Allies to help increase the financial literacy and planning skills of those who are ready to permanently change their lives.

Relevant Education

Employers often say they can't fill positions because of a dearth of qualified workers. Additionally, alternatives to traditional education pathways could fast-track individuals to be qualified for the current and emerging workforce. At Circles USA, educational leaders are accelerating opportunities through a curriculum for children that ensures a two-generational approach to ending poverty for young people and for their parents/guardians.

Cross-Sector Partnerships for Job Creation

Businesses, foundations, and government agencies need to invest in the hard-to-employ population. Otherwise, in many communities across the nation, businesses cannot grow to full capacity. There are not enough qualified workers to fill vacancies as well as potential new jobs. Circles USA has had success receiving capacity-building grants from Walmart, Green Mountain Coffee Roasters, Sun Bank, the Annie E. Casey Foundation, and Mass Mutual, among others. With more than 500 foundations, corporations, and government agencies investing in local Circles chapters, we are piloting and scaling ways to foster cross-sector partnerships for job creation.

Research, Data, and Accountability

We must regularly measure progress reducing poverty rates. At Circles USA, a new online data system tracks the increase of income for our families, plus 30 secondary indicators of success, such as reliable transportation and secure housing. We intend to track participation of volunteers, too. Through research, we can further aggregate common challenges that families face, and we can scale solutions to those problems throughout the system.

Increasing Poverty IQ

Stories that dispel stereotypes and inform people about what it really takes to move from crisis to prosperity are crucial to increasing the Poverty IQ of our nation. As Transformational Leaders, we use storytelling to inspire others to join the cause of poverty reduction.

Communicating Your Vision

In *Leading Change: An Action Plan from the World's Foremost Expert on Business Leadership,* John Kotter states that leaders must spend 70% of their time leading.[6] The primary task is communicating the vision to stakeholders in as many ways and times as necessary. Leaders underestimate the frequency of communication needed to create a new culture.

What are the elements of an effective communication of your vision? Here's insight from Carmine Gallo's *Talk Like Ted: The 9 Public Speaking Secrets of the World's Top Minds*:

1. Unleash the master within.
2. Master the art of storytelling.
3. Have a conversation.
4. Teach me something new.
5. Deliver jaw-dropping moments.
6. Lighten up.
7. Stick to the 18-minute rule.
8. Paint a mental picture with multisensory experiences.
9. Stay in your lane.

I highly recommend Gallo's book as a primer for amplifying your capacity to communicate your vision. What if you do not like public speaking? Or what if articulating a vision is not what you want to do all the time? It's important to understand your preferences now so you can identify the role that best suits your personality. To lead, one must have clarity about his or her role along with time dedicated to play it. Let's review your preferences, aspirations, and how you are currently spending your time.

---

[6] John Kotter. Leading Change: An Action Plan from the World's Foremost Expert on Business Leadership.

Are You a Visionary, Facilitator, or Practitioner?

All three roles, visionary, facilitator, and practitioner contribute to achieving the vision of ending poverty, and we each possess all three capabilities. The question is: Which one is most dominant for you, and how does that fact affect your leadership? How you communicate your vision will in part be informed by whether you identify as a visionary, facilitator, or practitioner.

Based on a military model adapted from a talk by Vipin Gupta, a colleague and a research physicist at Sandia National Laboratories, here is a description of the three types:

> **The *visionary*** says we need to take the hill. It's an impossible task to most, but the visionary makes the *impossible* seem *possible*.
> **The *facilitator*** prepares the hill to be taken. By negotiating with the visionary and translating the vision into action, she or he turns what's *possible* into something *probable*.
> **The *practitioner*** implements the day-to-day details for taking the hill. By collaborating with the Facilitator, he or she makes what's *probable* more *predictable*.

	Visionary	**Facilitator**	**Practitioner**
Purpose	Makes impossible more possible	Makes possible more probable	Makes probable more predictable
Example	We can and should end poverty!	How do we create an organization to do that?	How do we run the program?
Primary interest	Gaining agreement and commitment about what's possible	Building the organization to achieve the mission	Making things happen on the ground

Visionaries can see, often with great clarity, how the world could function after the transformation. Even in the face of many unknowns, visionaries have confidence that something new is possible. Facilitators appreciate the visionary's vision and can see it well enough to help make it a reality. Facilitators possess patience and enthusiasm to figure out the practical steps, so they can implement the plan. It is often a disaster to put visionaries and practitioners in the same room without facilitators, because a practitioner's questions might stop the flow of a visionary's process.

We all have habits that identify our preferences. A practitioner might say, "Just tell me what needs to be done." A facilitator might say, "I don't want to be in charge, but I can help organize things in the background." A visionary might say, "Let's do this completely differently."

Knowing what role feels best to you is important information. If you are not called to be a visionary, take heart, you can still lead a tremendous change. As a facilitator, you can seek out visionaries who need someone like you to translate their visions to others. If you are a practitioner, you can insist that visionaries and facilitators join the leadership team to play their roles.

Understanding the preferences of your teammates is equally important. If you plug people into the wrong roles, you will end up with unnecessary difficulties. Take the time to learn how to read people's interests and skills with regard to the roles of visionary, facilitator, and practitioner.

High-Impact Communication Strategy

How can you communicate your vision in a way that will motivate key players to align with that vision and to commit to help you bring it about? Who is in your sphere of influence, and how might you engage them in the most efficient and effective way possible?

Decide on the reach you want to have with regard to your forms of communication. If you are a visionary, you might be drawn to large social and news media audiences and should consider which outlets will give you the largest impact. Facilitator types might prefer working with organizational audiences and/or cross-sector teams. Practitioners might prefer to work in a coaching role with their leadership team and support them in expanding the vision through their own unique talents and preferences.

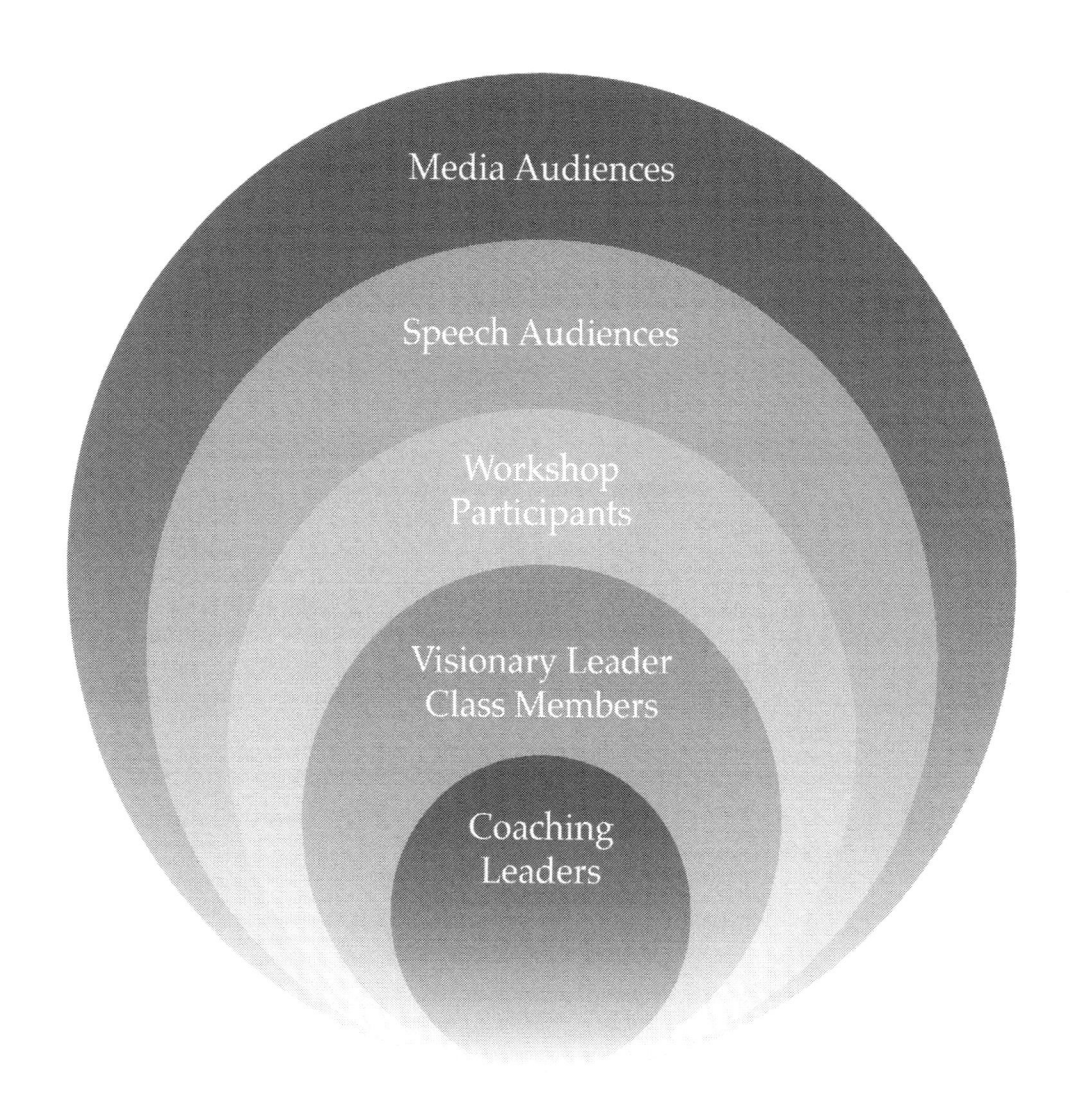

- Media Audiences
- Speech Audiences
- Workshop Participants
- Visionary Leader Class Members
- Coaching Leaders

Leading Versus Managing

Whether you are a visionary, facilitator, or practitioner, you need enough time to play your role. Each role must engage in the entire Transformational Map: articulating a vision to others, aligning with other leaders and facilitating a shared vision, helping yourself and others learn whatever is needed to achieve the vision, and building policies and program structures that will embed the vision into reality. Realistically, three to four days each week are needed to provide leadership to people through all four stages of the Transformational Map.

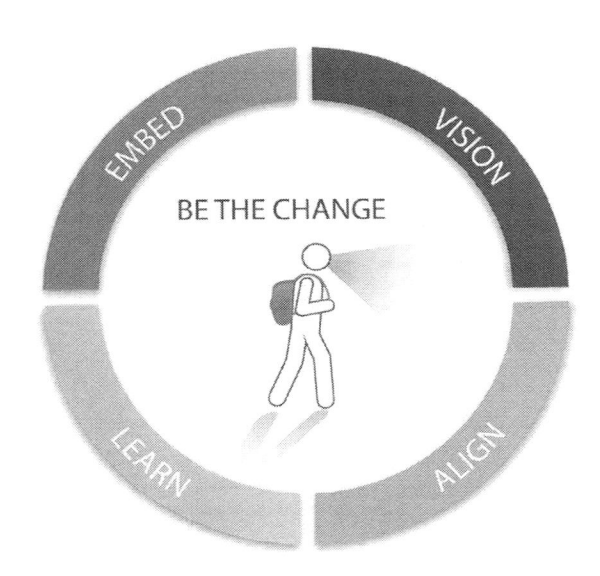

Many leaders find themselves saddled with management responsibilities. They are busy with budgets, personnel issues, and administration. If one is spending the majority of time in management, there is no way one can lead a transformational process to change the culture of an organization, a community, or a system. Sure, some management is unavoidable, but leaders must have time to read, write, think deeply about ideas, and then discuss those ideas with others. Leadership is needed in order to create a shared vision that makes people feel they can achieve something great.

Transitioning from manager to leader requires careful planning. The first step is to decide such a transition is important and then to find ways to delegate management to others. This might require reprioritizing budgets, raising funds to hire a manager, and letting go of low-impact programs. Remember, high-impact programs change the community's and organization's mind-set from poverty management to poverty reduction. Which of your current programs are doing that, and which are not? What can be done to either bring programs from low impact to high, or to eliminate programs in order to free up time and resources?

Scott Miller's Example of Preferred Future

The following excerpt is a vision of a poverty-free community that I wrote in my first book, *Until It's Gone: Ending Poverty in our Nation in our Lifetime*. It provides an example of a detailed vision of what I want the world to look like based on my values and deepest desires. Rather than focusing on an individual story, this is a story about an entire county. Its actual name is Story County, Iowa, home to the city of Ames and Iowa State University. It is where we first conceived the Circles USA approach in the late 1990s.

Ending Poverty by 2050

When I woke up on January 1, 2050, I joined my large circle of friends to formally celebrate the elimination of poverty from Story County, Iowa. Let me tell you how this happened. It's an amazing story that few believed possible 60 years ago.

Once we were sure that all our children were safe and healthy, then, and only then, did we turn our attention to making our personal lives more comfortable. Schools no longer charged fees for extracurricular activities. All children now had access to computers in the home so that the playing field was level from the beginning.

We helped couples decide to postpone having children. Adults made the conscious decision to slow down and take the time to really notice the extraordinary individuality of each child in our community. We decided to invest more of our time and energy in raising our children than in the pursuit of wealth. We got so interested in children that we were right there for them, in appropriately sensitive ways, on the very days when they had questions about sexuality, feelings of loss, and anxieties about being loved. We became more sophisticated about what children need from adults and made it our priority to give it to them. We watched while teen births gradually decreased, then became a thing of the past. During 2049 in Story County, no child was born to teenage parents.

Adult parents in Story County learned how to value maintaining a committed relationship above all else—how to simplify life by reducing unnecessary consumption, freeing up time and energy for building and strengthening their commitment. We realized that the benefits of having a successful, lifelong partnership far outweigh the difficulties we all experience sustaining one. People stopped tolerating emotional and physical abuse—indeed, the community developed strong, assertive plans to interrupt patterns of abuse in families. Men and women realized the necessity of establishing good relationships with one another in order to stay close. People got better about asking friends for help with negotiating the challenges of staying together and raising a family. Children observed these changes and so learned how to choose compatible mates and how to communicate effectively to maintain a good, intimate relationship. The rate of family breakups fell from 50% to 6%.

Employers in Story County saw the wisdom of turning away from short-term earnings, investing more time and money into building teams of steady, reliable, well-paid workers able to fully utilize their talents to provide meaningful services to the community. During the past 40 years, employers have shifted away from generating products and services of questionable value for people and the environment, moving toward a deep commitment to enrich lives, while conserving and renewing natural resources for future generations.

Health insurance became universally accessible, benefiting thousands of vulnerable families in Story County. Many of the county's older residents still remember the years of preferential medical care; younger people hear those stories with disbelief.

Transportation changed as radically here as in the rest of the nation. Electric vehicles replaced the fleet of polluting cars we once had. Supplementing our clean energy supply by natural gas burning facilities is necessary less than 5% of the time. Electric bus service now extends to all area businesses and communities. The use of bicycles increased dramatically as it became safer and easier to pedal around the county on hundreds of miles of newly constructed bike paths. As generosity and making new friends became a normal way of life, carpooling became easy. People with lower incomes now don't have to worry about maintaining a car. There are plenty of ways to get where they need to go. Those who absolutely need a car but can't afford the price can obtain a donated vehicle that has been donated.

The cost of housing decreased dramatically during the past 40 years. No one now has to spend more than 30% of take-home pay for rent. The city of Ames and Story County, through a number of bold public initiatives, paved a clear and reasonable path for anyone to move from affordable, subsidized rental situations to home ownership.

Because adults focused more on children, Story County citizens enthusiastically created the best childcare support system we could. Iowa joined the rest of the states in providing excellent and affordable childcare for all. Most people had more time to spend with their own children because of their commitment to staying together as families, and, as life became more affordable and manageable, they didn't feel compelled to work ever longer hours.

Story County developed such a powerful social safety network that it became virtually impossible for anyone to suffer poverty in isolation. These emergency financial support services have become just as important to us as our emergency police and fire services. People in our communities now know when families are in financial trouble and so are able to reach out quickly and effectively before evictions, job losses, family breakups, and a host of other destructive outcomes occur. Every community has ample emergency funding, plenty of skilled volunteers and professionals who know how to intervene, and Circles USA to ensure that people don't fall back into poverty. A family's financial crisis is treated as an opportunity for community members to reach out in service to a neighbor—to support a family out of isolation. We have realized that every member of the community has gifts to share, and we've stopped wasting human potential by marginalizing individuals and families living in poverty.

When I woke up on January 1, 2050, I realized that at some point during the previous 40 years, a critical mass of people had figured out how to have enough money, enough friendship, and enough meaning in their lives to be truly happy. This core group became the catalyst necessary for making it an eventual reality for all. Story County had been transformed.

Back to the Present

My vision might or might not become a reality. It's really up to us. I am committed to reaching the goals outlined in this book, and so are many others. You can make a big difference in someone's life. It is possible to eliminate poverty.

May peace be with you: May your children inherit a thriving Earth, may your neighbor rise safely out of poverty, and may you find more happiness than you ever thought possible as you collect enough money, enough friends, and enough meaning in your life to make you smile your way through the rest of your day.

Questions for Reflection

1. What breaks your heart? Which of your non-negotiable values are being violated in the world?

2. What is your case for why we need a new system to end poverty, including both the pain of the unjust present and the promise of a preferred future?

3. Take time to reflect on the mission statement for your organization and make notes here about where it resonates and where it feels disconnected from your non-negotiable values.

4. Consider your case for change and for a preferred future in the context of families, your community, and your organization:

Case for change	Preferred future in three years
Families:	Families:
Your community:	Your community:
Your organization:	Your organization:

5. With regard to developing high-impact strategies, please review how you are spending the majority of your time and resources. Rank each strategy using the chart.

Strategy/Activity	Impact	Change required to increase impact

6. With regard to being a visionary, facilitator, or practitioner — which is most dominant for you?

7. Are you managing or leading? Review your typical week's calendar and explore where you can delegate.

Management and low-impact activities	Possible solutions

8. How do you organize your life to "be the change" in alignment with your larger goals?

9. At what percentage are you ready and willing to accept the call to end poverty? If the number is anything less than 100%, even 99%, but not 100%, then what do you need to know or do before you become ready to accept the call?

10. Comment briefly on your leadership style. Have you had experiences of inner delay patterns and/or giving up on others prematurely?

SECTION 3: ALIGNING WITH OTHERS

> When people align around shared political, social, economic, or environmental values and take collective action . . . the lives of millions of people around the world can truly change.
> —Simon Mainwaring

Gaining Agreement and Commitment
Circles of Agreement

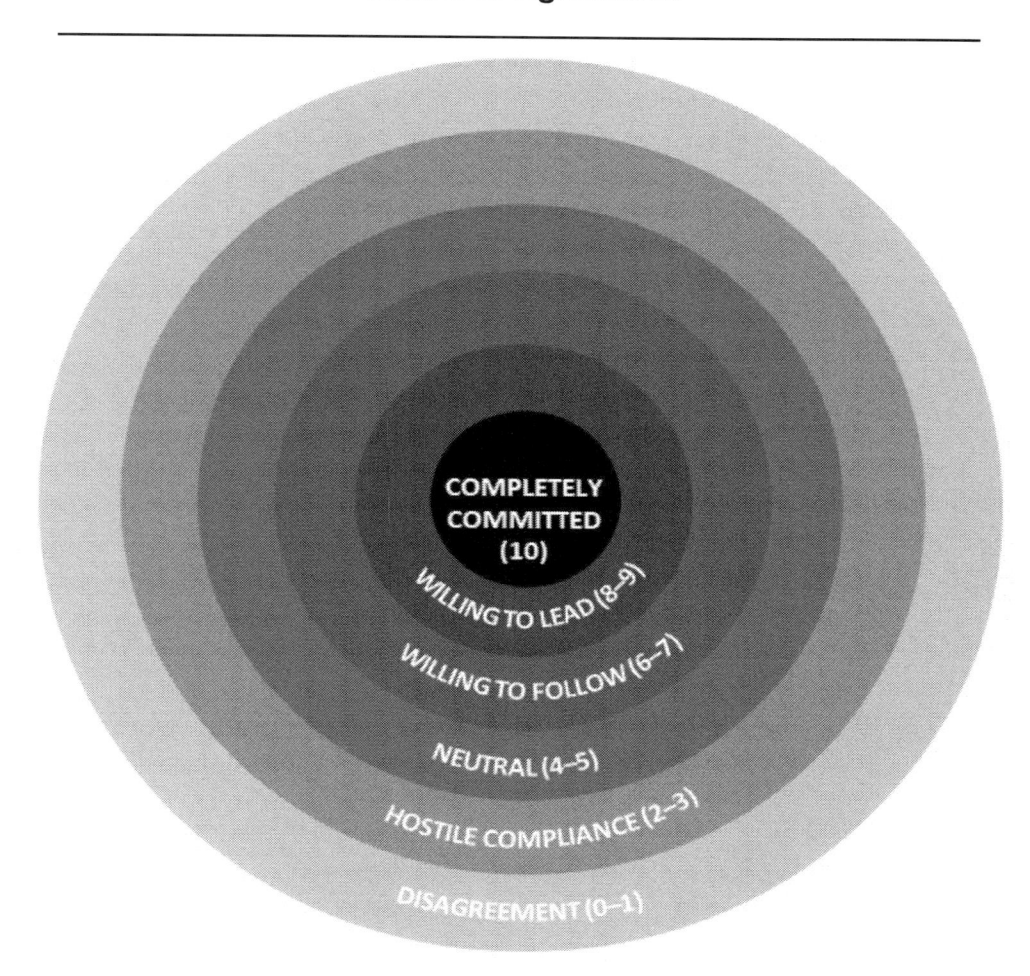

- COMPLETELY COMMITTED (10)
- WILLING TO LEAD (8–9)
- WILLING TO FOLLOW (6–7)
- NEUTRAL (4–5)
- HOSTILE COMPLIANCE (2–3)
- DISAGREEMENT (0–1)

The Top Management Team(s)

A fully empowered leadership team is aligned to a shared vision and works together to move others through the process embodied in the Transformational Map. Each knows his or her role and has enough authority to carry out his or her responsibilities. She or he must also be aligned with her or his own organization's top management team.

The team at the top of an organization must be analyzed to determine its capacity to lead transformational change. Standing committees, ad hoc committees, and de facto leaders and groups who have "always done things the same way" can become siloed in their approach to meeting the organization's mission and its new change agenda. In order to implement the change that is envisioned, the way in which work gets done must change to align with the new strategies. Here are examples of how the leadership team must evolve as it moves into the various stages of the Transformational Map.

Before	After
Top management team members manage grants, finance, or technical management areas, spending little time leading.	Top team members are leaders, managers and community deal makers.
Top managers have little reason to plan together or coordinate activities; they meet seldom.	Top team must continuously focus together on organization strategy implementation, meeting often.
Managers spend very little time in the community developing relationships and partnerships; community has little knowledge of organization.	Top leadership team members are community deal makers, engaging the community around organizational strategies,
Teams are not often formed anywhere in the organization.	Teams form around strategies; every staff member is on a team.

The defining criterion for membership in the top leadership team is the ability to fulfill a staff member's role in supporting the transformational change process.

Practices and Procedures

Leaders must analyze existing practices and procedures to assure alignment with the change initiative.

Definition: Practices and procedures are the way policies and strategies are carried out in the organization or system. They might develop formally or informally over time. They might be invisible — we don't notice many of them because they are "the way we do things around here." Some are in writing, some are not. Leaders and managers usually have the authority to change them without changing policy.

Examples: performance review, communication systems, staff development, leadership development, recognition systems, compensation systems, budgeting processes, purchasing, planning work activities with individual workers, and many others.

Exercise: Identify the key structures, practices, procedures, or organization attitudes that will hinder your organization from moving through the transformational map:

You should now have an outline for the organizational shifts that must occur for you to align your leadership efforts to achieving the vision. Management should be firmly delegated to others, and the leadership team should focus on articulating the vision, gaining agreement and commitment from stakeholders, facilitating learning, and embedding change into the culture.

Archetypal Roles in Organizations

Several leaders we work with like to use the following court roles as a metaphor. To be effective, organizations must have strong people playing the roles of King/Queen, Warrior, Lover, and Wizard.

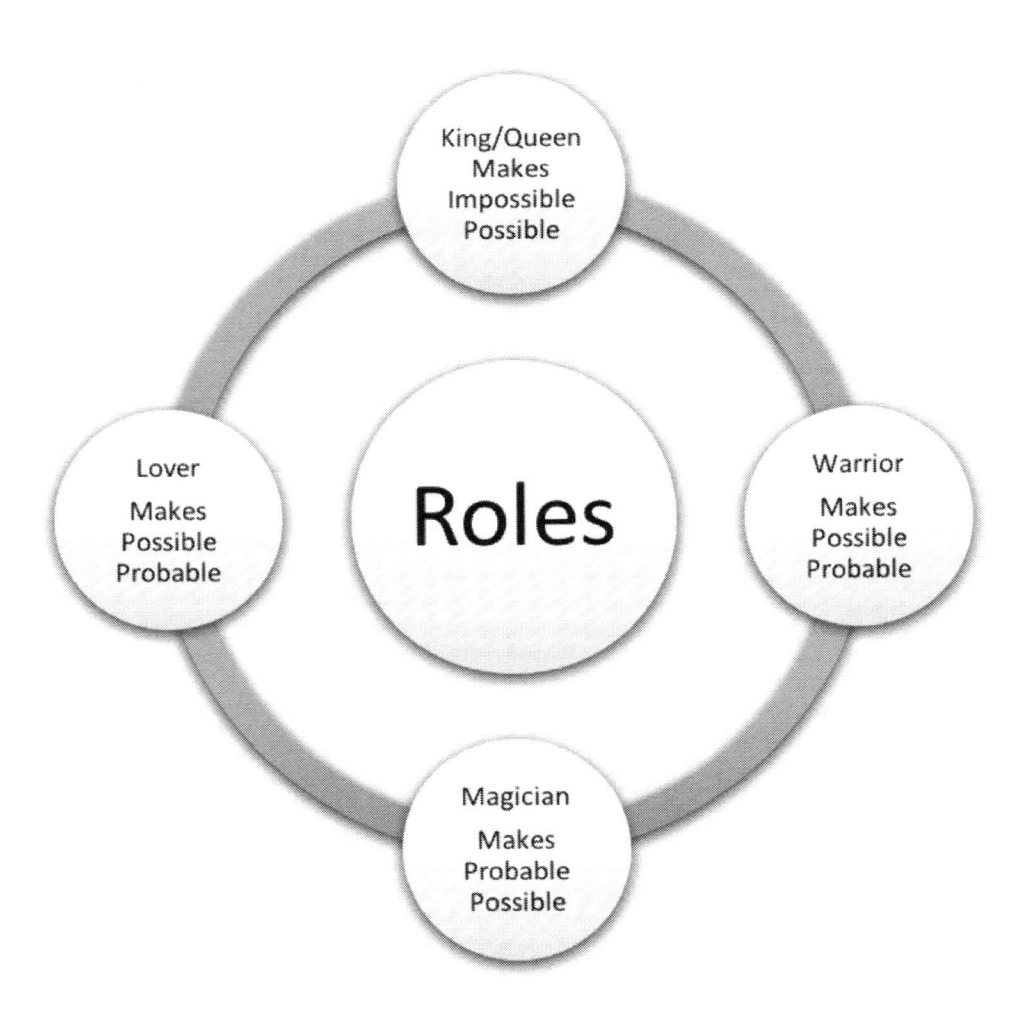

- King/Queen: Makes Impossible Possible
- Warrior: Makes Possible Probable
- Magician: Makes Probable Possible
- Lover: Makes Possible Probable

King/Queen

The primary responsibility of the King or Queen is to download the initial vision and communicate it regularly to others so that it can be built upon through a shared vision involving the key stakeholders of an organization or community. John Kotter, author of *Leading Change*, speaks to the importance of creating a sense of urgency. The Queen or King cannot underestimate how frequently she or he needs to articulate his or her vision and eventually the shared vision. In most organizations, the King or Queen is played by the CEO, president, or executive director. In collaborative leadership, it can be an entire group of leaders who are playing this role in tandem with each other.

Warrior

Every organization is vulnerable. Its weaknesses must be monitored and addressed by the Warrior. Unexpected threats arise, and it is the role of the Warrior to take responsibility to protect the organization. Too often this role is left to the King or Queen, which is inappropriate. It is too difficult to effectively lead and protect at the same time. The Warrior role is typically played by the CFO, executive assistant, and/or COO. His or her job can also include protecting the King or Queen from himself or herself as needed. Obviously, there is a strong level of trust between Warrior and Queen or King.

Lover

Lovers are the ones who attract others to the organization. They typically work in sales, fundraising, marketing, communications, and community engagement positions. Lovers are those you want to be around, join with, and have ongoing interactions with throughout a process. They are very easy to get along with and will go out of their way to help you.

Wizard

The Wizard develops and maintains the magic that an organization creates in products and services. He or she is the one generating the *value added* for the world. The Wizard(s) can be the chief technology officer, services or products manager, chief designer, etc. Because the Wizard is producing on behalf of the organization what the world is buying, it is easier for the Wizard to confuse his or her role with the King or Queen than for the Lover or Warrior. When and if that happens, the King or Queen must immediately assert his or her role and reset the boundaries to eliminate confusion.

The more able we are to understand these personality traits in ourselves and others, the easier it is for us to build a conscious leadership team that is capable of functioning at a high enough level to bring about transformations. Does your organizational leadership team possess each of the archetypal roles: King/Queen/Warrior/Lover/Wizard? If not, how can you bring someone onto your team to play these crucial roles?

Building a Shared Vision

The transformational planning process builds a shared vision that generates more commitment and solutions than you had before you started. To transform something requires a clear vision of what life would be like as a result. You must make this visioning process very personal for those you want to engage in your agenda. You must engage Allies in a rich planning process that taps into both their deepest worries and their dreams for the future. You will create strategies for creating the next level of commitment from stakeholders to the shared vision.

There are three reasons to involve others in developing your transformational plan:

1. To have a **shared vision**. Peter Senge and other experts on organizational development tell us how rare it is to find a truly shared vision.
2. To generate commitment. Shared visions generate more **commitment** than visions that are passed down from above. People find activities more meaningful if they are involved in developing those activities.
3. To create better strategies. The more people enjoy pursuing the vision because it is personally meaningful to them, the more insights and energy you have going toward getting results.

Your **preparation** for developing a transformational plan is now complete. You developed a clear leadership agenda in Step 1. You have recruited a leadership team, and you have gathered compelling data. You are now ready to engage the community, your staff, and board in the transformational planning process for the purpose of building a shared vision that generates more commitment and solutions than you had before you started. So, what should the plan look like when it is done? How will you know if you have something that is really capable of transforming your community?

Now, it is time to start writing the plan that will guide you and your stakeholders over the next couple of years. Here are the most important points to consider when writing your plan:

> 1. Make it highly readable. Use "language of the heart" to capture people's attention and to remind them of your passion to achieve the vision.
>
> 2. Make it specific, holding people accountable to leadership assignments that will make a clear difference.
>
> 3. Continue revising your drafts until you can reach consensus with your stakeholders. Have them show it to others who will be playing a role. Even if it takes 20 versions, it will be worth it to get full buy-in.

Another tip is to have one key writer who is supported by someone with editing and planning skills. Let these two people synthesize the feedback you receive. Much of the feedback will be about outcomes and strategies. One rule of thumb with outcomes is that they should challenge the stakeholders of the plan without setting them up for failure. You don't want your staff, program participants, board members, or volunteers feeling bored because the indicators are too modest or feeling anxious because they are too ambitious. Regarding strategies, the dialogue needs to be around two questions:

1. Do we have the right criteria to evaluate the potential impact of our strategies?

2. Do we have the highest impact strategies we are capable of implementing?

Criteria for a Transformational Plan

Circles USA took 100 leaders of community action agencies from Missouri and Kansas through a nine-month planning process organized around the steps described in this book. In preparation for their final transformational plan documents, we asked them to develop criteria that would distinguish a plan as **transformational**. They developed the following list:

> - Bold, energetic, visionary, innovative, addresses ending poverty
> - Integrated, holistic
> - Long range, long term
> - Simple, understandable
> - Clearly defined, high impact strategies
> - Measurable, clear, high impact outcomes
> - Data driven
> - Engaging to the community

Your plan must boldly address your target issue. The strategies you choose must integrate services to fit the people being served in a holistic manner. These strategies as well as the outcomes you are pursuing through them must be clearly defined. You must choose strategies that you predict will have a high impact on changing the beliefs of the community, thereby bringing about changes in goals and rules that affect your target population. The plan must engage your organization and the community for at least the next three to five years and must include a simple and understandable vision of how the world will be different as a result of your work. Accurate and relevant data should drive your process and guide your decision making. And, finally, you are not going to make significant societal change unless you engage the community in doing it. No organization can function as the lone ranger and expect good results.

Self-Reflection Questions

1. If I already belong to an organization that is in alignment with my vision, what influence do I have to bring about my specific vision?

2. Are there additional organizations that I could join, partnerships that I could create, or resources I could access to help achieve my vision? If I were to join them, how much more influence could I have in the world?

3. What seems to trigger the biggest procrastination patterns in me? And how can I discontinue those patterns?

4. As I think of my impact in this world, what must I release for my vision to come into being? What must I embrace?

People Hear the Call to Adventure Differently

For the past 40 years, I have met countless everyday heroes who have heard the call to alleviate the suffering caused by poverty. Heroes who have big hearts, keen minds, tenacious personalities, compassionate ears, generosity beyond the norm, and an uncommon amount of common sense. I have been inspired by the thousands of everyday heroes who have humbly answered the call to adventure and forged new relationships with people who have either a lot more or a lot less money than they do. People join our work with Circles USA because they want to help someone else. The nation has a deep tradition of charity, goodwill, and a love-thy-neighbor attitude, and it is wonderfully evident throughout our network of Circles USA chapters across the country and in Canada as well.

How one hears the call to adventure is influenced by one's belief system about how the world operates. In early 2001, a national poll conducted by National Public Radio (NPR), the Kaiser Family Foundation, and Harvard University's Kennedy School asked nearly 2,000 Americans aged 18 or older, "Which is the bigger cause of poverty today: that people are not doing enough to help themselves out of poverty, or that circumstances beyond their control cause them to be poor?" Respondents were roughly equally divided between "people not doing enough" (48%) and "circumstances" (45%).

A 2016 poll conducted by the *LA Times* and the conservative think tank American Enterprise showed similar results in terms of who or what is responsible for poverty — but with interesting nuances. For example, White blue-collar workers were more likely to blame the poor for their situation than Whites with college educations. When it comes to solutions, the study showed that more Blacks than Whites believed that government programs put people back on their feet and allowed them to get jobs and out of poverty. A majority of Whites believed that government programs create dependency and encourage people to stay poor. People in poverty believed that government programs fail primarily because not enough money had been put into them. More affluent people than working-class people believe that government programs are badly designed.

When people first get involved in Circles USA, they usually have a strong set of opinions about why people are in poverty and what kind of help they need. What happens through their experience with Circles USA, however, often shifts these opinions over time more to the middle ground. Many people discover that it is the combination of self-responsibility and planning skills coupled with new support systems and better designed private and public programs that can best help people escape poverty.

Because people do not change their belief systems easily, and because our beliefs ultimately drive what we do as individuals, a community, and a nation about poverty, the *beginning of the end of poverty* must start with understanding our current beliefs. While we have books and training programs that can increase people's awareness of their beliefs, the most important strategy of Circles USA is the opportunity to build healthy and effective relationships across socioeconomic class lines. We want people in poverty to get to know people of middle-income and upper income means. It is through these relationships that people challenge their assumptions and arrive at better, more informed views of poverty.

As a White suburban kid, my primary call to adventure was to chase the American Dream as defined by making money, buying a nice house, raising a family, taking fun vacations, and having a respectable career. I learned that shopping is good for the economy, more stuff equates to more happiness, and respect from others comes through higher income and net worth. While my parents were born during the Great Depression and had a deep respect for the value of a dollar, my surroundings screamed out to me that consumerism is the path to happiness. My worldview might have remained the same except that I fell into an emotional abyss trying to be an architecture student, a path that did not seem to be my calling or fit my talent. Through the confusion that followed my leaving the architectural program, I encountered several significant guides who challenged my thinking to its core.

In my mental model of the American Dream, people could make as much money as they wanted to if only, they applied themselves. Through this lens, I saw the United States as the greatest equal opportunity nation on Earth. It was a level playing field, and if you worked hard and played by the rules, you would inevitably achieve the promises of the American Dream. Being poor was largely the consequence of not putting enough effort into one's goals. Enabling the poor with subsidies, for example, was not going to help them in the long run.

Four Common Responses to Poverty

The call to adventure to address poverty typically comes in one of these four ways:

1. Please provide private, limited charity to deserving, needy people as prescribed by my faith.
2. Please mentor someone poor who wants to learn how to not be poor anymore.
3. Please directly hire the poor.
4. Please support any policy that would eliminate subsidies that ultimately enable the poor to stay poor.

What's wrong with solution No. 1, charity to the deserving poor?

Nothing is wrong with charity per se. *Expecting that it will solve the long-term problem of someone experiencing poverty is the problem.* The major issue with charity is that most people expect it to solve the underlying problem, which typically backfires because of a dynamic identified by Dr. Stephen Karpman as the "Drama Triangle." My first job in the "anti-poverty" field was to meet with up to 40 people a week who were coming in asking for handout of $50 to $100. In 15-minute interviews, it was impossible to discern whether the financial assistance would help or hinder in the long run. Furthermore, I had no place to refer people so they could address the underlying reasons for being in poverty. It was this experience with charity that eventually led me to the development of Circles USA.

When the call is that of charity, we are compelled to see someone as a "deserving victim" who can be rescued, at least in this moment, with a quick fix of some sort. We do not engage with the complexity of the situation, instead prescribing the fix(es): Let me give you some food, a check, gasoline, or a referral to someone else who can help some more. I might be involved with a program that can help you get a job, repair your car, be a better planner, manage your budget, etc. Our unwillingness and often inability to acknowledge that poverty is complex for both internal and external reasons leads us down a path of disillusionment when our help doesn't seem to add up to a long-term result. We might begin to harbor feelings of resentment toward the person who refused to be fixed through our "wise counsel" and best intentions.

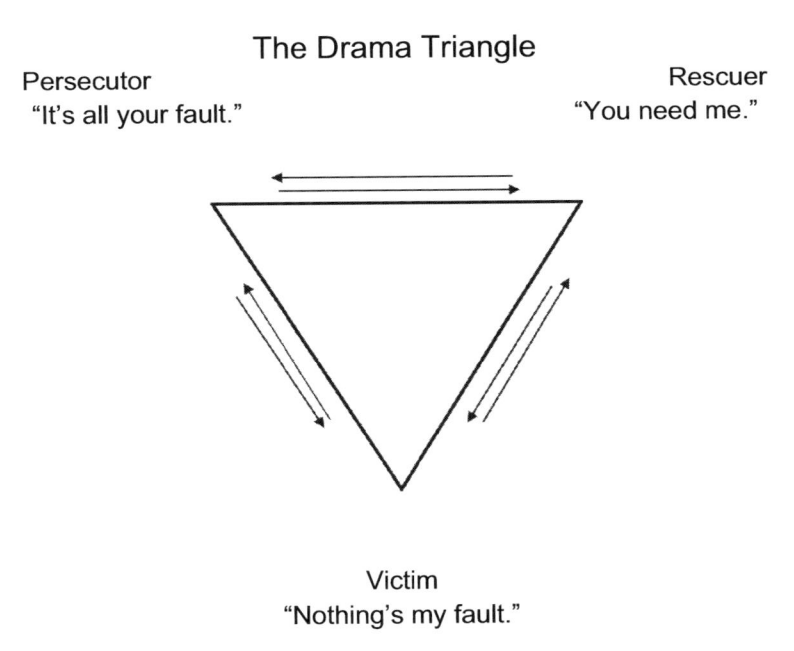

The Drama Triangle

Persecutor
"It's all your fault."

Rescuer
"You need me."

Victim
"Nothing's my fault."

Persecutor: Appears controlling, critical, angry, authoritative, rigid, and superior.

Rescuer: Needs to be needed. Enables others to remain dependent and gives them permission to fail; rescuing helps rescuers avoid facing their own issues.

Victim: Appears oppressed, helpless, powerless, ashamed—finding it difficult to make decisions or solve problems.

The Drama Triangle addresses individuals' perceptions as they shift back and forth between roles. The drama persists when it fulfills some unmet need for individuals to continue in conflict in lieu of addressing the real issues, identifying solutions, and taking action.

Books such as *Toxic Charity* and *When Helping Hurts* have become popular study group material in faith communities as they examine their own experiences on the Drama Triangle. Circles USA is attractive to faith communities because they see it as a structured and safe program through which to build long-term relationships of mutual respect that begin to address the underlying problems of poverty. We call the participants in Circles USA who are working their way out of poverty Circle Leaders in order to reinforce the idea that they will make their own plans to move out of poverty and tell others how they would like to be supported. It puts the rescuer impulse on its head.

What's wrong with solution No. 2, mentoring the poor?

The problem with the second solution, *mentoring the poor*, is that it begins with the assumption that people with middle-income and upper-income means and backgrounds know enough about the experience of poverty to tell people in poverty how to effectively address the challenges of being poor in our nation. Nothing could be further from the truth. People in poverty must inform all the decisions that go into making their own personal plan, as well as the development of community and government programs that are designed to "support the poor." Without the wisdom of such a partnership, middle-income and upper-income folks fail with spectacular consistency as evidenced by an unchanged poverty rate for decades and decades of well-intentioned government and charity efforts. The result of these failures, unfortunately, is often to simply blame the poor: "We have great anti-poverty programs, we just need better poor people."

The first person I ever tried to help out of poverty resisted my first 38 great ideas to fix her. The more enthusiastic I was to find a way to fix her, the less willing she was to invest her time in interacting with me. I wanted her to take my advice and get out of poverty. Our relationship ended immediately and for good reasons. I had a low poverty IQ, unrealistic expectations, no support system to determine how best to be of assistance, and a worldview that she definitely did not share. Life did not look like endless opportunities for the taking to her. It looked hostile, disappointing, and dangerous. Her everyday challenge was one of survival. Mine was a search for more meaning through making a difference to another. I was willing, just sadly uninformed.

What's wrong with solution No. 3, just hiring the poor?

Nothing, as long as employers have at least a higher-than-normal poverty IQ. We often hear, *I gave them a job, and they didn't show up on time, in uniform, with a smile, ready to work. They were ungrateful, unreliable, and my business suffered for trying to be helpful.* Again, the Drama Triangle is in play. *We are giving people what they want and need, but they are blowing it.*

There are a couple of new economic realities that make strategy No. 3 something that employers must undertake if they are to sustain and grow their businesses. In the book *When the Boomers Bail*, my friend and colleague Mark Lautman shows clearly how the massive exodus of aging baby boomers from the workforce now forces employers to mine the talents of their "unqualified workforce" to fill jobs. When there were plenty of job candidates, communities and their employers could manage a consistent level of poverty because there were plenty of others to hire, and the economy could handle the costs of carrying a percent of dependents without much burden on the tax base.

In communities that now suffer from slowing economic development efforts through which they are unable to bring many new jobs to town, there is enormous pressure to increase the number of qualified workers and to reduce the tax burden of dependents in poverty. This *forced call to adventure* is a great opportunity for communities to finally see that solving poverty is not just a humanitarian effort—it has become an *economic development imperative*.

Stanford University published a case study about Cascade Engineering, a business in Grand Rapids, Michigan, that found success with an innovative approach to hiring people from welfare. I had the opportunity to visit them and speak with owner Fred Keller about his insights into what it takes to successfully employ, retain, and advance the poor:

    1. An accepting organizational culture.

    2. Education, not only of new employees but also of existing employees, about what it means to be in poverty.

    3. A strong system of support for people moving from poverty into careers.

The results? Keller and his company improved their welfare-to-work program results from a 29% retention rate per year to over 90%.

Fred is now one of the investors of our Circles USA chapter in Grand Rapids. He sees the value of building long-term relationships between those who need jobs and those who can support people in finding, keeping, and advancing in those jobs over time.

What's wrong with solution No. 4, simply dismantling subsidy programs?

Finally, the idea of simply dismantling subsidy programs in an effort to stop enabling people to stay in poverty is promoted as the ultimate quick fix to dependency. Unfortunately, as compelling as this might sound to conservative ears, *reducing poverty is more complicated*. Let's review the key causative factors of poverty that emanate from each of the six major sectors of society—business, government, education, human services, civic and faith, and philanthropy—and what their call to adventure for reducing poverty rates might be.

When I contemplate how well our nation is doing compared to other nations, I look at global metrics that go beyond a simple GDP number. In the Declaration of Independence, the pursuit of happiness is defined as a fundamental right, as long as you don't do anything illegal or violate the rights of others. Using this fundamental right as the main metric, how is the United States doing?

The Organisation for Economic Co-operation and Development (OECD) is a group of 34-member countries that discusses and develops economic and social policy. OECD members are democratic countries that support free-market economies. Their first World Happiness Report was published in April 2012 in support of the United Nations high level meeting on happiness and well-being. Since then, OECD members have come to see happiness as the proper measure of social progress and effective public policy. In June 2016, the OECD committed itself "to redefine the growth narrative to put people's well-being at the center of governments' efforts." The six variables for the index are income, healthy life expectancy, having someone to count on in times of trouble, generosity, freedom, and trust, with the latter measured by the absence of corruption in business and government.

In 2007, the United States ranked third on the happiness index for OECD nations. In 2016, it had dropped to 19th (out of the 34 OECD nations) due to an increase in corruption and a decrease in social safety nets. At the top of the happiness index were the Scandinavians for the opposite reasons. George Lakey, author of *Viking Economics: How the Scandinavians Got It Right—and How We Can, Too*, explains in an easy-to-understand manner how the Nordic nations emerged at the top of the Happiness Index, as well as in these other important categories: freedom of the press (measured by Freedom House, the United States ranked 26th); best place to grow old as measured by Global Watch Index; and life satisfaction as measured by OECD.

The OECD also does poverty rate comparisons across the 34 nations. Iceland ranked No. 1 with the lowest poverty rate, followed by Denmark, Czech Republic, Finland, and Norway. In the No. 30 spot was the United States, followed by Israel, Brazil, Costa Rica, and China. I don't know about your reaction to this list, but my mind jumped off the rails when I read it.

Most people in the United States know, and perhaps take pride in the fact that our GDP is $18.56 trillion, far and above second-ranked China at $11.39 trillion, and third-ranked Japan at $4.73 trillion. Our per capita income ranks fourth, behind Luxembourg, Norway, and Switzerland, according to OECD data. It's interesting to note that overall GDP does not correlate positively with lower poverty rates or higher happiness indexes. Being a wealthier nation also does not translate into being safer. According to Nation Master, China is ranked 12th out of 189 nations for highest homicide rates, and the United States is ranked 14th. In other words, you are less likely to be slain in 175 other nations than in the United States.

Wealth disparity is running twice as high and broad in the United States as in any other industrialized nation. The top 5% own more than 90 times the wealth of the median household. In the second-ranking nation, the top 5 % in the Netherlands owns 42 times the wealth of the median household. What is the factor for the happiest place on the globe, Norway? Twelve times. Is there a correlation between a national value of equity and happiness, lower poverty rates, higher productivity? As Lakey says in book, *Viking Economics*,

> Like most Americans today, Norwegians a century ago didn't like the results of a wealth gap: the hunger and poverty, the crime, elderly friends warehoused or left in isolation, young people without hope of a good job. Norwegians also didn't like the attitudes that went with inequality: an inclination toward arrogance among higher-income people and the feeling among lower-income people that they were losers, defeated by the system.

The Nordic model has been promoted by many in the United States who want to see more equity and less poverty. It has been demonized by others who feel strongly about the free-market system and limited government. The polarity between right and left media, politics, and arguments within one's own family has accelerated as more people find themselves unable to participate in the American Dream. But the United States is not just one nation with one long history of people who share common values, beliefs, and ancestries. No, we are a hot mess of people from at least 11 different ethnic origins who have been fighting for control of the White House, Supreme Court, and Congress for the past 240 plus years.

Why the Call to Adventure in the United States is Complicated

Colin Woodard wrote a beautiful book titled *American Nations, a History of the Eleven Rival Regional Cultures of North America.* He answers the question, "Why do Americans have such a difficult time agreeing on basic issues like the meaning of freedom, the role of religion in public life, or what it means to be an American?" His primary answer is that we were settled by 11 separate nations, giving each of these diverse regions of the country their own distinguishing ideals. Colin's book is a brilliant page turner, and I am not going to spend much time reiterating what he says. What I want to point out is this: To reduce poverty rates in America, we must understand the distinct beliefs of each region.

I was raised in what Colin calls the Midland region, which, he says, is arguably the most "American" of the 11 nations. The region was founded by the English Quakers around the values of pluralism and organized around the middle class. ". . . government has been seen as an unwelcomed intrusion and political opinion has been moderate, even apathetic . . .," he writes.

The Midlands region stretches from its roots in the Delaware Bay throughout Middle America and the Heartland, comprising Pennsylvania, Maryland, southern New Jersey, northern Delaware, central Ohio, Indiana, Illinois, northern Missouri, most of Iowa, and the eastern halves of South Dakota, Nebraska, and Kansas. It includes the cities of Chicago and St. Louis. People in this region largely believe society should be organized to benefit ordinary people; are skeptical of top-down government intervention; and are considered to hold the standard American political viewpoint, containing the key "swing vote" in every national debate. The Midlands functions as a powerful mediating force, agreeing with only some of its neighbors' more extreme views.

I am very much a Midlander, having lived in Pennsylvania from the ages of 4 to 9. We then moved to Rochester, N.Y., the region that Colin calls Yankeedom. This region was founded in Massachusetts Bay as a religious utopia in the New England wilderness. The emphasis was on education, local political control, and the pursuit of the greater good of the community. Yankees believe, more than any other region, that government can improve lives and galvanize their resistance to aristocrats, corporations, and any other outside power. Also, very much me. Yankeedom stretches across upper New York State, northern strips of Pennsylvania, Ohio, Indiana, Illinois, and Iowa, parts of the eastern Dakotas, Michigan, Wisconsin, and Minnesota.

Hopefully, this brief summary has whetted your appetite to look at Colin's book and identify your own region's roots. He argues that it is very difficult to change the belief system of a region. In fact, people tend to migrate to regions where they feel an affinity. He has mapped out the regional identity of all of the 3007 U.S. counties, which on the one hand is helpful although overall his ideas pose a challenge to reducing poverty rates. The Call to Adventure to address poverty has to be messaged with different talking points, depending on regional belief systems. While it would be so much simpler to characterize the conflict between red and blue states, it is obviously nuanced by regions and then within individual states in those regions. In fact, from community to community along the borders of Colin's map of the nation, ideologies can be vastly opposed to one another.

In a future chapter, I will discuss the Bootstraps and Benefits dialogue and provide some thoughts on how people from very different orientations can work together to reduce poverty rates. We are unlikely to change our worldviews easily, but working with people who hold diverse political and religious beliefs for a common goal of supporting people out of poverty is a good starting place for maturing our narrative regarding the ultimate roles and responsibilities from each of the major sectors of community life. Here is a summary of shifts that we need to make:

EXAMPLES OF SECTOR SHIFTS FOR SUSTAINABLE ECONOMIES THAT ELIMINATE POVERTY

Sector	Unsustainable & Increases Poverty	Sustainable & Decreases Poverty
Business	Focus on profit as only bottom-line. E.g., environmentally-degrading farming and energy practices; resistance to livable wages. Elimination of jobs through automation, artificial intelligence, globalization, and ineffective baby-boomer transfer of their businesses and wealth to others when they retire.	Focus on triple-bottom-line—e.g., B-corporations that align policies and procedures with consideration to profit, planetary impact, and the wellbeing of employees and customers Workforce development aimed at sustainable industries and careers. Smart retirement and business transfers that keep jobs and wealth in communities.
Government	Transactional programs focused on managing compliance while providing services and benefits in silos. Any policy that inhibits hard working people from being able to meet their basic needs and save for the future, e.g., Cliff effect problem that doesn't incentivize work.	Funding community-based solutions that use relational strategies and transactional programs together to support people completely out of poverty. e.g., Circles and Poverty Reduction Labs

Sector	Unsustainable & Increases Poverty	Sustainable & Decreases Poverty
Education	Emphasis on content, teaching styles, rules and regulations that are no longer aligned with the skills, content, and agility required of the emerging economy Lack of emphasis on earning and managing money	Working closely with economic development agencies in order to determine skills and content required to succeed in the emerging economy Financial education from an early age that emphasizes budgeting, savings, and investments Teaching styles that align with students' different learning styles and interests
Health and Human Services	Random services targeting health symptoms rather than underlying causes Random services to address aspects of poverty	Focus on prevention through behavioral changes in lifestyle that promote health Coordinating services with long-term, comprehensive programs that lead to economic stability Empowering people to develop and achieve their own goals, manage their money, and expand their social networks for better opportunities
Civic	Random community projects with a focus on short-term assistance Emphasis on using community work to proselyte or enroll members into one's' group.	Emphasis on relational-based community service that creates a stronger, more empowered community that can thrive

Sector	Unsustainable & Increases Poverty	Sustainable & Decreases Poverty
Philanthropy	Short-term, quickly changing investment strategies that keep grantees busy pivoting in order to receive funding High churn rates in staff that lead to disruption in program strategies and grantee relationships.	Long-term comprehensive investments with emphasis on relationship-building and technical assistance that increases capacity of grantees to utilize high-impact strategies

The Call to the Business and Education Sectors

Just as there was no stopping the Industrial Revolution, there is no stopping what is happening next with automation, globalization, and artificial intelligence. The composition of jobs in our economy is never going back to the way it used to be, and this fact has major ramifications for poverty rates. The top of the "food chain" in our communities is, for better or worse, the business sector. It wields the most influence on all other sectors. This was not always the case in U.S. history, but it is now.

In October 2011, I did a TedX talk. In that speech I said that poverty should be understood as an economic development problem, not just as a humanitarian problem to be fixed by nonprofits. The emerging economy is not just one of many factors affecting poverty rates; it is perhaps going to have the biggest impact of all potential factors. By 2030, half of all jobs could very well be entrepreneurial in nature. The opportunity to be on someone's payroll in a traditional w-2 job is rapidly diminishing. Companies can generate wealth with far fewer people than ever before. For example, according to the Brookings Institute, in 2014 Google was valued at $370 billion with only 55,000 employees, a tenth the size of AT&T's workforce in the 1960s.

The key characteristic to possess in order for anyone to survive, let alone thrive, in the emerging economy could be the ability to be nimble. While there are arguments about whether automation and artificial intelligence will displace millions or will generate new jobs to employ the displaced or will have very little impact on employment rates, there is significant concern about where things are heading with our economy and what we should do about it.

Flexicurity is a term first used in 1995 to describe a partnership between business and government to support the citizenry as the economy continues to morph and destabilize current jobs. If it is possible for the majority of goods and services to be delivered (droned, even) to our homes through a handful of super corporations such as Amazon, who buys the goods and services with what money from what jobs? A closed system must be kept intact between makers and consumers. A pure-market system economy could very likely create this closed system with fewer people, leaving a significant portion of the population on their own to survive. Taken to extremes, a Darwinian order sorts out the weak from the strong.

Fortunately, the United States is already using a hybrid economic system that mixes big multinational corporations with big government deterrents and incentives with an independent sector of for-profit and nonprofit organizations, as well as black marketplaces that provide every imaginable good and service. Our economic sector is a complex system of forces that regulates infinite variables that result in how we personally experience economic freedom and security. Because the complexity is mind-boggling, the desire to over-simply solutions to sell to the mass public for political and financial reasons is strong. The desire to repeal and replace Obamacare, for example, affects one-sixth of this massive economy. As I write this, Congress is finding it increasingly difficult to find the votes to repeal it and replace it with something else that can be presented in a sound bite to the American public as a better alternative.

The Call to Adventure for the economic and education sectors is to look around the globe and learn. It is time for us to let go of the arrogant notion that we are the best nation on Earth, and therefore we should be mentoring everybody else, end of story. Far from it. As I suggested, the new global metrics of happiness, low crime, low poverty rates, and high life satisfaction tell us that we are losing ground to nations that are getting smarter about their economies and educational systems.

Paul Poler, CEO of the massive multinational corporation Unilever, wrote an editorial that was featured in the *Huffington Post* in July 2014. I have excerpted portions of this radical and optimistic call to adventure to the business community. It is worth reading the entire editorial. The following excerpts reinforce my assumptions about what the true call is for the economic sector:

"It was Winston Churchill who famously said that 'democracy was the worst form of government apart from all the others that had been tried.' Much the same can be said for capitalism, particularly the form of capitalism that has been practiced over the past 20 years. . . .

". . . capitalism, with all its faults, is the only game in town. The task confronting the present generation of leaders is to improve on it, to build on its strengths and eradicate its weaknesses. . . .

". . . Addressing the weaknesses of capitalism will require us, above all, to do two things: first, to take a long-term perspective; and second, to re-set the priorities of business. . . .

"... The requirement to report back to investors every ninety days distorts behavior and priorities. It is absurd for complex multinational companies to have to invest huge amounts of time preparing detailed income and margin statements every quarter. ...

"... The priorities of business also need to be challenged. Since the 1980s we have all been worshiping at the altar of shareholder value. This is a doctrine that says that the principal purpose of business is to maximize returns to its investors. ...

"At Unilever we have challenged both these precepts. We have abandoned quarterly reporting as well as guidance. We have also made it clear that our paramount goals are to satisfy the demands of consumers and customers and to serve the needs of the communities where we operate. I am convinced that if we do these things well, we will deliver excellent returns to our shareholders. And so far, we have not been disappointed, as we have performed strongly despite a challenging economic environment. ...

"... If business is to regain the trust of society, it must start to tackle the big social and environmental issues that confront humanity, especially at a time when governments seem increasingly to be caught in shorter and shorter election cycles and have a hard time internalizing the global challenges in an increasingly interdependent world. As I have said many times, 'business cannot be a mere bystander in the system that gives it life.' The environmentalist Paul Hawken believes that if there is any deficit we are facing right now, it's a deficit of meaning. Many are talking about the need for a GDP+. A broader measure of success than just simply measuring wealth creation . . ..

"... For Unilever, these are to be found in addressing the needs of billions of people for clean drinking water, basic hygiene and sanitation, nutritious food and sourcing all of our agricultural raw materials sustainably. ...

"... When people talk about new forms of capitalism, this is what I have in mind: companies that show, in all transparency, that they are contributing to society, now and for many generations to come. Not taking from it. ...

"... It is nothing less than a new business model. One that focuses on the long term. One that sees business as part of society, not separate from it. One where companies seek to address the big social and environmental issues that threaten social stability. One where the needs of citizens and communities carry the same weight as the demands of shareholders. ..."

The bottom line cannot just be quarter-to-quarter gains. The B-Corps movement in the United States is gaining traction with the formal adoption of a triple-bottom line: profits, people, and planet. From the B-Corps website: Collectively, B Corps leads a growing global movement of people using business as a *force for good*. Through the power of their collective voice, one day all companies will compete to *be best for the world*, and society will enjoy a more shared and durable prosperity for all. When it comes to reducing poverty rates, my bets are on the influence of this and similar movements.

The Call to the Human Service, Government, Civic, and Philanthropic Sectors

People working in the other four major sectors of society will forever feel as if they are losing ground on the resolution of poverty because we have a poverty management system rather than a poverty reduction system. The individual responsibility to get out of poverty and become economically stable is sabotaged by the responsibility of a system that is not accountable to reducing poverty rates. We need to build an alternative system that incentivizes getting out of poverty. A poverty reduction system works in tandem with business and economic development programs to ensure we have enough people prepared for the opportunities within the emerging economy.

The most important contribution to be made by leaders in these four sectors is to intentionally build alternative poverty reduction systems that allow teams of paid and volunteer workers to support groups of people out of poverty and into sustainable jobs. The following graphic shows that these teams will support people long enough to reach the finish line of the race out of poverty.

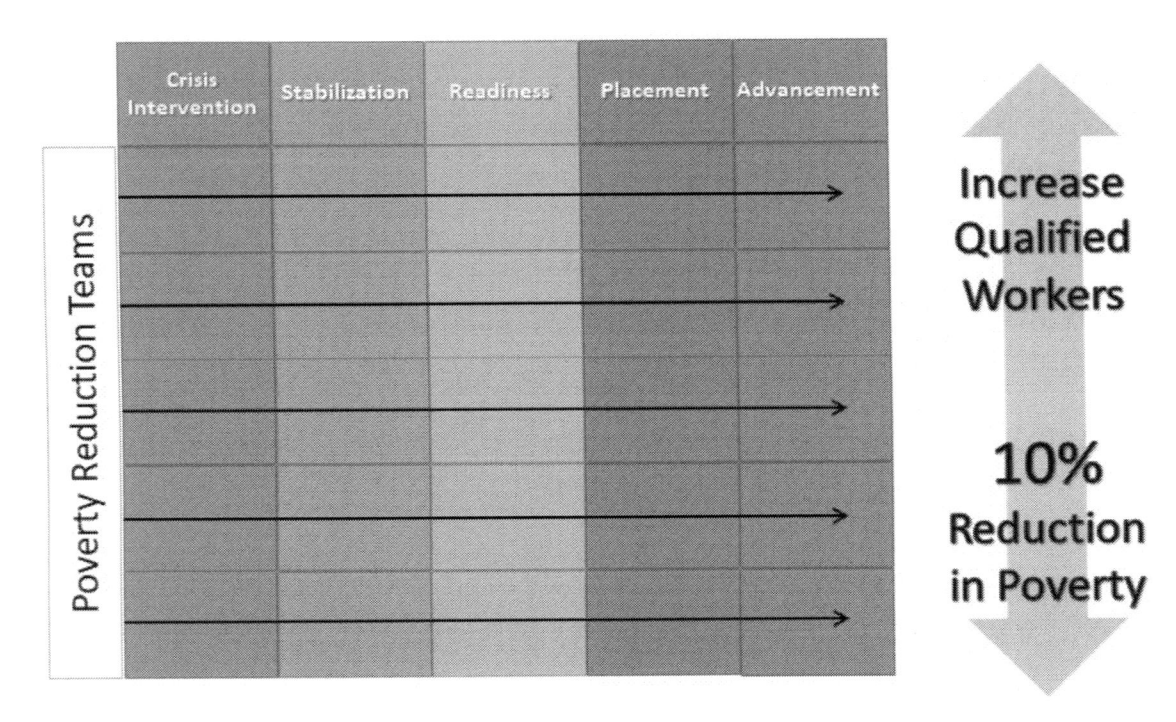

Linking the Poverty Reduction System to a Job Creation System

E > P*

Your vision for a sustainable community must include the formula E > P, meaning your community's economy must grow faster than your community's dependent population (those too young, too old, or too unqualified to work).

What does sustainable mean?

1. Jobs and careers that pay enough income to meet household needs and then some
2. Careers that are relevant in America's emerging economy
3. Employment that contributes to a sustainable environment
4. A commitment to live within one's means
5. A community culture of doing what is best both for the community and for the individual

Once you have a clear assessment of a sustainable economic future, you need a strong plan for how you are going to prepare your community for it. Follow the TAPUMA* steps:

Think: Get a coherent understanding of your poverty reduction and job creation systems.
Assess: How many sustainable jobs do you need in order to have full employment? What are the system barriers and service and programs gaps that you need to address to get to full employment?
Plan: How do you proceed?
Underwrite: Who pays for your plan?
Manage: How do you manage your progress in achieving your vision?
Account: How do you meet the expectations of your underwriters and other stakeholders?

*Courtesy of our colleagues at Community Economics Lab; visit: thecelab.org.

Undergirding the Poverty Reduction System with a Relational Strategy

A Poverty Reduction System will need to include a powerful relational strategy in order for people to take full advantage of transactional programs. Relational strategies strengthen the social capital of people who want to move out of poverty and into economic stability.

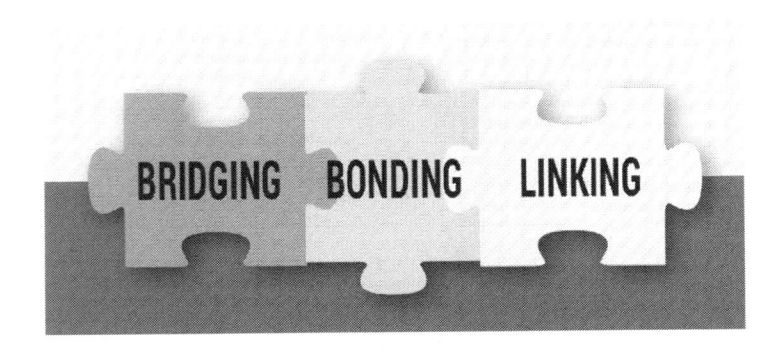

Bridging capital builds relationships across socioeconomic class lines, which is important for helping people understand the middle-class rules for success in education, networking, employment, financial management, and career advancement.
Bonding capital builds peer-to-peer relationships that provide motivation, support, and important information in achieving economic stability.
Linking capital builds relationships between community service programs and individuals who want to use them effectively.

All three types of social capital are necessary in moving out of poverty.

Any Poverty Reduction Team will need some level of all three types of social capital. Teams can create a Circles USA program specific for their needs or refer into an existing one. Once a job creation plan is in place, Poverty Reduction Teams can be organized along specific career pathways, utilizing Allies who have successfully worked in that career.

Building an Intentional Community to Reduce Poverty

Building all three types of social capital requires diligence to support people through the four stages of any successful relationship.

In the honeymoon phase, people have inspiring but unrealistic expectations based on some form of the Drama Triangle, e.g., I will be rescued, I will rescue, etc.

The disillusionment stages occur as reality pushes back on these fantasies, and people start to feel disappointed when their expectations go unmet.

The insight stage is the building of a more realistic and productive relationship.

The working stage is the continued deepening and strengthening of the relationship over time, which leads to achieving mutual goals.

Building a Productive and Appreciative Culture

What allows people to move through the four stages of relationship building across socioeconomic class lines and achieve goals? Building a community culture that includes effective ground rules and rituals, which follow:

> Open meetings with New and Goods—personal good-news item that gets people thinking positively and sharing some parts of their life, which makes it easier for others to connect to them over time.
>
> Finish meetings with appreciations that acknowledge something positive about others and increases the sense of belonging and esteem of all members.
>
> Give everyone at least six mistakes a day so that they are willing to take risks to build new relationships without worrying about making mistakes. Normalize the inevitable stepping on each other's hidden rules and help one another to forgive and forget.

Poverty Reduction System Teams

Team	Composition	Role	Responsibility
Leadership	Primary Leader and highly committed sector leaders	To lead the PRL process	Share vision, gain alignment, secure and allocate resources, facilitate learning, and embed changes into the culture
Administrative	Primary leader and support team	To manage the PRL and support the teams as needed	Manage meetings, logistics, communication, and budget
Planning	Planners from stakeholder groups across sectors	To solve systemic problems to reduce poverty	Use CQI to test scalable solutions to system barriers and service gaps identified by Poverty Reduction Teams and report to Leadership Team
Poverty Reduction	Collaborative teams comprised of caseworkers and others who can build a long-term relationship with people moving out of poverty	To support households in moving out of poverty and to identify system barriers	Build long-term relationships and support households through all five stages of economic stability; identify and report service gaps and system barriers to Planning Team

The Call to Adventure from Circles USA

Poverty is both immoral and economically unstable for families, communities, and our nation. We can eradicate it if we decide to commit ourselves to a long-range plan to do so. There are tipping points that can help us reach critical mass if we use solutions that address both the internal and external challenges of moving out of poverty. For example, we need to have an effective relationship strategy that is coupled with realistic pathways to more income. A workable strategy cannot exist in just a few communities; it must be scalable in order to significantly reduce poverty rates. Circles believes that reducing poverty rates by at least 10% can engage tipping points that would begin the end of poverty.

Joining others to end poverty is an exciting, courageous, and noble journey to take. You will be challenged and transformed as you embrace the unknown waters of new relationships with people from different economic backgrounds. You will gain deeper insights into the underlying problems of poverty and have a real opportunity to solve both individual and systemic causes. You are guaranteed to learn something new about yourself and the world. You will be changed for the better. And you will have a unique opportunity to help others live an exceptionally improved life.

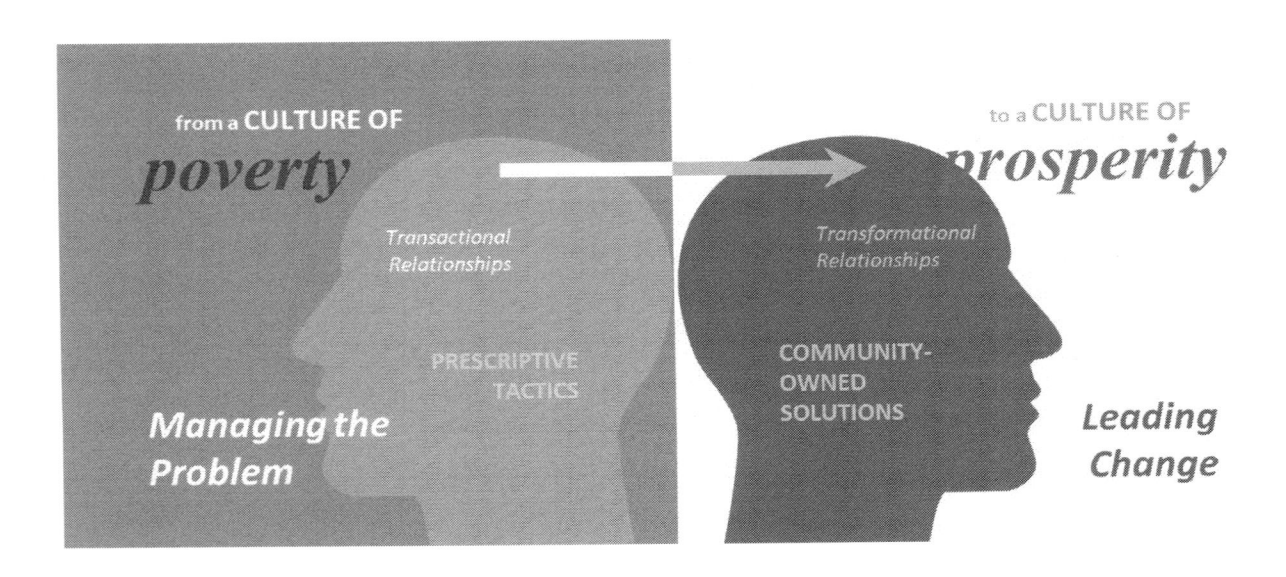

from a **CULTURE OF** *poverty* — *Transactional Relationships* — **PRESCRIPTIVE TACTICS** — *Managing the Problem*

to a **CULTURE OF** *prosperity* — *Transformational Relationships* — **COMMUNITY-OWNED SOLUTIONS** — *Leading Change*

Tips for Aligning One's Own Job and Life to the Vision

What is Your Story?

WHAT YOU WANT

Your Story Creates Your Future

WHAT YOU DON'T WANT

If you want to predict your future, listen to your conversations. What story are you telling yourself and others? Are you taking yourself and others into the future you want—or the future you don't want?

Your vision must be connected to your deepest core values. If it is not, then you will not have the motivation and sustained energy to see a transformation through from beginning to end. Ask yourself, "What must happen in the next three years?" Ask it about your own life as well as about your community.

Once you articulate a vision that is highly important to you, you are ready to translate it into stories that move others toward achieving the vision.

We connect with one another emotionally, first, and then with information, second. Feed what you want to see happen with your story. Remember that a storyline that complains about how systems, people, events, community, and so on don't work will only perpetuate a negative future. The power of self-fulfilling prophecy is real. Are you telling a story that leads to what you want or what you don't want?

In the spirit of being the change, it is helpful to ask the following questions:

1. What in your life do you want to change so as to align to your new vision? Think about what we have discussed—people, activities, and your environment.

2. What support do you need from others in order to make the change?

3. Are you ready? On a 10-point scale where 10 represents the highest level of readiness, how ready and willing are you to change your life in ways that are most important to you?

4. If you are not a 10, what is between you and being a 10?

5. Now that you have identified the resistance, are you ready to let it go and take immediate action to begin your plan? What steps will you take this week?

Aligning the Environment

> Look around at the clutter and chaos you are tolerating. Now picture it organized. Won't it feel wonderful?
>
> -Mary Sigmann

Mary is a personal organizer and long-time friend of my wife and me. When we first met, I hired Mary to help me declutter my office. What I learned from her was a set of organizing principles that I still use to this day:

- Only have around what you need to use to achieve your most important goals.
- Clutter distracts and siphons away valuable energy.
- Make tomorrow's next step inviting by preparing for it today.
- Your environment should be your ally, not your adversary.

In my office, I have a clutter-free desk to use as a primary workspace. I have another desk that I use to organize projects as I work on them. I keep paper at a minimum and do whatever I can to eliminate unnecessary clutter. I have my own personal art and photographs on the walls to enjoy and to remind me to include my own creative works in my next projects. I have only the books I use for reference or inspiration on my shelf. The rest have been given away. I go through my office space every quarter and clear out the old so I can bring in the new.

We downsized into a new home that has a wonderful flow to it and will support both of us in feeling more relaxed, alert, and inspired to make the most of each day. We have given away or sold everything we no longer need or want. By having only those things in our environment that serve us now, we are reminded to do the same with our activities, relationships, and thinking. Our space is functioning as an Ally to achieving our visions.

So, it is time to ask yourself: How does your environment support your work as you achieve your vision? What would make it better?

TIP: Invite someone who is really good at organizing to come over to your home and office and give you a fresh perspective on what he or she sees.

Aligning Everything Else

As we explore the stage of alignment, more insights will come to us regarding how we can bring our relationships, our environment, and our activities into finer alignment to achieve our vision. Simply continue asking yourself, "What do I really want?" Our inner voice can guide us if we stop paying attention to our mental chatter and listen to it.

Here is a sample list of things in my life that I am in the process of aligning to my new vision:

- Diet—emphasis on local, natural, and vegetarian
- Exercise—more biking and walking
- Entertainment—fewer videos and movies for entertainment—less is more—money in my pocket and time to be involved with my community of friends and neighbors
- Neighborhood—moving into a neighborhood of less expensive homes, closer together, and with a higher level of neighborliness. Becoming a better neighbor by spending more time with others
- Money—reducing core expenses to a minimal amount and spending more money on donations for high-impact causes
- Travel—less use of planes and cars—more biking, day trips, and use of internet technology to connect with clients and long-distance family and friends

Self-Reflection Questions

1. Are you as organized as you want to be?

2. Does your environment act as an Ally, helping you to stay focused on the most important leadership assignments? How is it distracting you?

3. What can you do immediately to reduce clutter?

4. What are your long-range plans to declutter everything that does not serve you anymore?

5. What system can you put into place to remain clutter free?

SECTION 4: FACILITATING LEARNING

> Live as if you were to die tomorrow. Learn as if you were to live forever.
> —Mahatma Gandhi

When Moses caught his vision of a promised land and then aligned the masses to join him, he had to lead them across the desert. Metaphorically, this story illustrates the four stages of the Transformational Map. The promised land is the vision, the followers of Moses aligned with his vision, the desert refers to the learning agenda required to achieve their vision, and the arrival at the promised land is the final stage when we embed the vision into the culture.

Our worldview, skill sets, and life experiences will provide invaluable guidance and support, but the vision will demand personal learning from us. You have to ensure that those who are helping to achieve the vision are able to learn whatever is necessary to do so.

Self-Reflection Questions

- What do you personally need to learn in order to realize your new vision?

- Specifically, what skills, information, and new habits must you learn in order to achieve your vision?

- In order for others to share your vision, what must they know? Interview others, and then craft a learning agenda for achieving your vision in the world.

Refining your Personal Learning Agenda

We are each having a certain level of impact on the world around us. The Transformational Leadership approach assumes we are ready and eager to make a more significant impact in order to bring about the vision for our life and the world we want.

Upon further exploration, my inner voice told me more about my personal learning agenda:

I need to regularly clean out the mental clutter and hone my ability to laser-focus on my priorities. The move to my smaller home cleared clutter from my environment. Moving to four days a week with Circles USA freed up time and energy to focus on activity that is in alignment with my emerging new vision. Writing this book is reinforcing the ideas that are most important to me at this time in life. My new project with Transformational Leadership is a bridge to a more authentic experience and expression of self. I am learning how to be happier and more effective.

The following "curriculum" might work for your next stage of development as well:

1. Affirm and act on your personal freedom in each day and in each activity.
    a. Ask yourself regularly, "What do I want to do? Are there any "shoulds" I can identify and clear away?
    b. Measure success by the amount of time and joy spent on meaningful activity versus how much money is made.
    c. Change routines by inserting new and adventurous activity that generates more joy and enthusiasm for life.
2. Develop structure to increase accountability to pursue high-impact strategies.
    a. Commit to developing and following through on a strategic plan for both Circles USA and Transformational Leadership. Ask colleagues to help you stay focused on the plan, changing course only by intention, not through any delay pattern.
    b. Build regular check-ins with those who also like to stay on track.
    c. Do the essential but sometimes uncomfortable work of a clear and courageous evaluation of our weaknesses, unhelpful default patterns, and shadow selves. This might involve interviewing loved ones or trusted colleagues or working with a counselor. Including a plan to address "opportunities for growth" only strengthens our personal power. Keeping an open heart and the courage to be humble makes us better leaders.
3. Clear out the clutter in relationships and activity.
    a. As soon as it becomes clear that a client is no longer in alignment with achieving the transformational vision that you are pursuing, let go, and align with those who are.

b. Each week assess which activities produced the most joy and which did not. Commit to creating a more joyful set of activities for next week.

Self-Reflection Questions

- Ask yourself again—and this time tuning into your heart a bit more deeply—what do I need to learn next in order to increase my capacity to change my life and change the world?

- How can my Allies help hold me accountable to continuing my journey and achieving the milestones I have identified?

- Who knows me well enough to provide loving but honest feedback?

- What do I find most personally challenging, and do I know anyone who is accomplished in areas where I know I have room for improvement? Am I willing to ask for support?

Other People's Learning Agendas

Additionally, those who align with our visions and participate in our programs will form their own learning agendas, so we must be prepared to help them find the right people who can facilitate their learning. They will first need to understand best practices elsewhere that might be implemented locally. What training programs and support systems can be tapped into to help them learn their new roles? Secondly, they need to learn what they personally must know, be, and/or do differently in order to play their roles effectively.

Facilitating the Learning Curves

> Tell me and I forget. Teach me and I remember. Involve me and I learn.
>   -Benjamin Franklin

People learn in different ways. Some of us are predominantly aural learners, some are visual learners, and others are kinesthetic. We also all fall somewhere on the spectrum of introvert to extrovert. We might prefer learning in large group settings, in small groups, or alone. A variety of subjects might be more or less interesting than a deep dive into a single topic. Because of these differences, the more ways in which we provide learning opportunities, the more powerful our transformational group can become.

Circles USA has developed numerous ways in which we facilitate learning for all of our stakeholders to help us achieve our vision of ending poverty.

These include

1. Providing an online data system that tracks the progress of results and reports to stakeholders.
2. A website that provides general information about Circles USA and how to get involved.
3. An internal newsletter sent to our members.
4. Monthly webinars on topics requested by our members.
5. Peer-to-peer chat lines.
6. Monthly coaching calls with certified national trainers.
7. Annual conferences.
8. Regional and statewide events.
9. Development of new curricula each year.
10. Online folders where members can access templates for best practices.
11. A research and development process to test out new ideas.

12. Outside evaluators and annual board of directors reviews to integrate learning into our strategic planning.

Our learning will deepen as we proceed, and so will our vision. We are aligning ourselves with new people who will stimulate different perspectives and expand our worldview. It is important to keep coming back to the inner dialogue and do a gut check for what feels right to integrate into our Transformational Leadership Program. It is also important to consider how we will know whether we are making progress in achieving our vision.

The New Metrics of our Vision

As our new vision emerges, we have to ask ourselves these questions: What are the most important metrics around which we are going to organize our learning? How do we know we are moving closer to our vision? Obviously, our feelings are one source of guidance. But sometimes, discomfort is being generated by a delay pattern that needs to be released rather than by assuming the difficult feeling is an indication that we are on the wrong path. How do we know the difference?

Allies! Talking about our feelings with those we trust is the best way I know of to clarify the source of the feelings and to act accordingly. Writing down our thoughts is another way to understand why we are feeling the way we are.

No matter what we do, feelings always integrate, and we will naturally feel better in time. There is nothing to worry about when it comes to uncomfortable feelings. They simply provide you feedback.

However, feelings are not the only way to know we're achieving our vision. Every project has some desired outcome, something that can be measured and compared, benchmarks that can be noted.

As I review my new vision of sustainable, poverty-free communities, the first cut of metrics includes assumptions about what constitutes a tipping point to generate transformation. What comes to mind for me is this:

> *Progress will be measured by the amount of change I can inspire and equip leaders to make in the world. The most important changes will be measured by the latest and best metrics available in the field of sustainability. Ensuring a healthy ecosystem is imperative for the evolution of humanity.*
>
> *The economic system must be aligned to protect the bio systems that humans need in order to live and thrive. People who have the answers need an unusual amount of support to bring their changes to fruition. My role is to build a strong*

support system for myself first and then invite others to co-create their own strong level of support. Use what I have learned in Circles USA to build a group of Allies around my vision. Measure early progress by the number of people I can communicate with at each level of touch: social and general media, speeches, book sales, workshop attendees, and those I connect with one-on-one.

SECTION 5: EMBEDDING CHANGE

> When cultural change succeeds, it succeeds because it's so embedded in what we do that we don't have to think about it.
> -Harvey V. Fineberg

> Environmental concern is now firmly embedded in public life: in education, medicine and law; in journalism, literature and art.
> -Barry Commoner

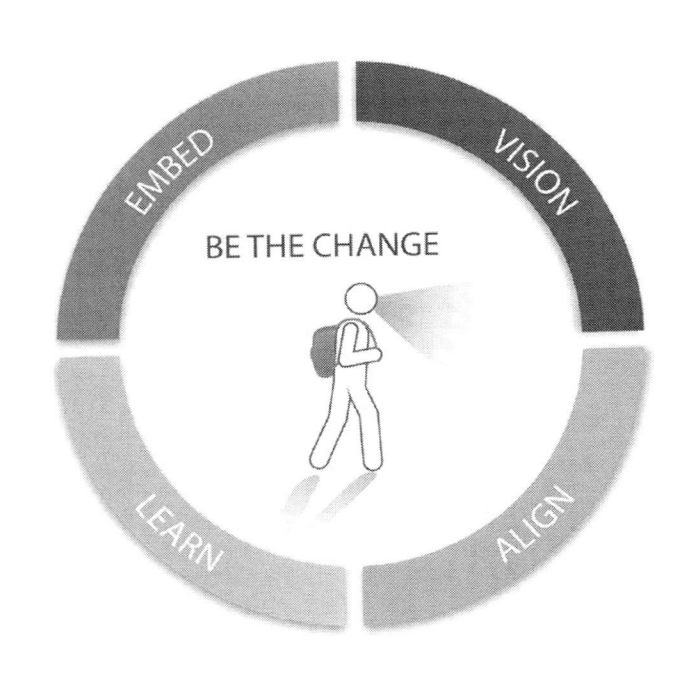

Embedding change into the culture requires formal changes in organizations, social and public policy, and a new generation of leaders who can carry the vision toward greater heights. To align people to nature in a way that we can predict will be sustainable for generations to come, we will need to listen to thought leaders regarding key structural changes that must occur.

Mental Model for Ending Poverty

As the Founder of Circles USA, I have a mental model for ending poverty. It looks like this:

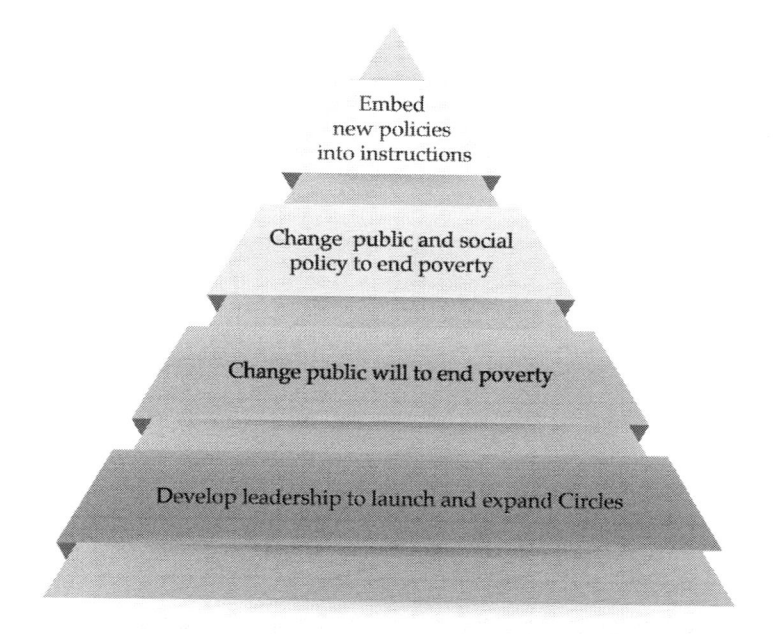

Embed new policies into instructions

Change public and social policy to end poverty

Change public will to end poverty

Develop leadership to launch and expand Circles

I am learning every day how to advance this model in order to achieve as much progress as possible toward an end to poverty.

The challenges of poverty intersect with the challenges of sustainability. Any policy that rewards overconsumption or risky behavior with the interaction of biosystems, such as carbon emissions, will erode future capacities to sustain life. Any economic policies that concentrate wealth into a smaller percent of the population will cause suffering for those at the bottom of the economic system because more money equals more power. With more money, the tendency is for wealthy people to isolate themselves from the general population and lose touch with the collective good.

People follow reward systems, which must be aligned to the new vision. What are the rewards of sustainability? As I listen to my inner guidance, here is what I hear:

An over-consuming economic system is exhausting. The addiction to spending money, acquiring more stuff, and the subsequent letdown from lack of deep fulfillment creates restlessness in every person affected. Once we have abundant proof of the information about the negative effects of overconsumption, serenity becomes the reward for simplifying our needs. This promise of serenity is what secures sobriety for those in the throes of addiction and is why 12-step programs have such success.

What are the New Structures of Sustainability?

To have a sustainable future, new systems will be formed in every sector of society. Although it is impossible to see all of the new structures that will result from pursuing the sustainability vision, embedding it in the culture will require radically different systems, including the systems that make up our economic, political, governance, and social realities. Those who have clarity about this vision will need to provide leadership.

Here are some examples of shifts that would support a more sustainable future:

Current	Sustainable future
Sustainability as a marketing device, providing only Band-Aids rather than addressing the long-term problems	Permanent changes in the production and delivery of goods and services in a manner that is in alignment with the capacity of Earth's biosystems
Consumption of meat at an enormous cost to the environment (water, deforestation, erosion, pollution, methane gas, etc.)	A shift to sustainable diets embracing alternative protein sources; teaching people how to cook; supporting "eat-local-foods" movement
Addiction to throw-away novelty items	A return to recycle, reuse, and repair habits that preserve products and reduce waste
Suburban sprawl and construction of large houses	Higher density and affordable housing
Continued concentration of wealth into the hands of fewer people, assuming that it will trickle down appropriately to everyone else	An economic system that allows all to meet their basic needs and then some
Increased healthcare costs with more expensive pharmacological and surgical cures	Holistic, lifestyle changes that are consistent with wellness and environmental respect

Unchanging Values

Articulating the values underlying our vision is also critical if we are to embed the transformation in the culture. The next generation of leaders must understand that there are non-negotiable principles that guide the future of maintaining the transformation.

There are the key values that undergird Circles USA:

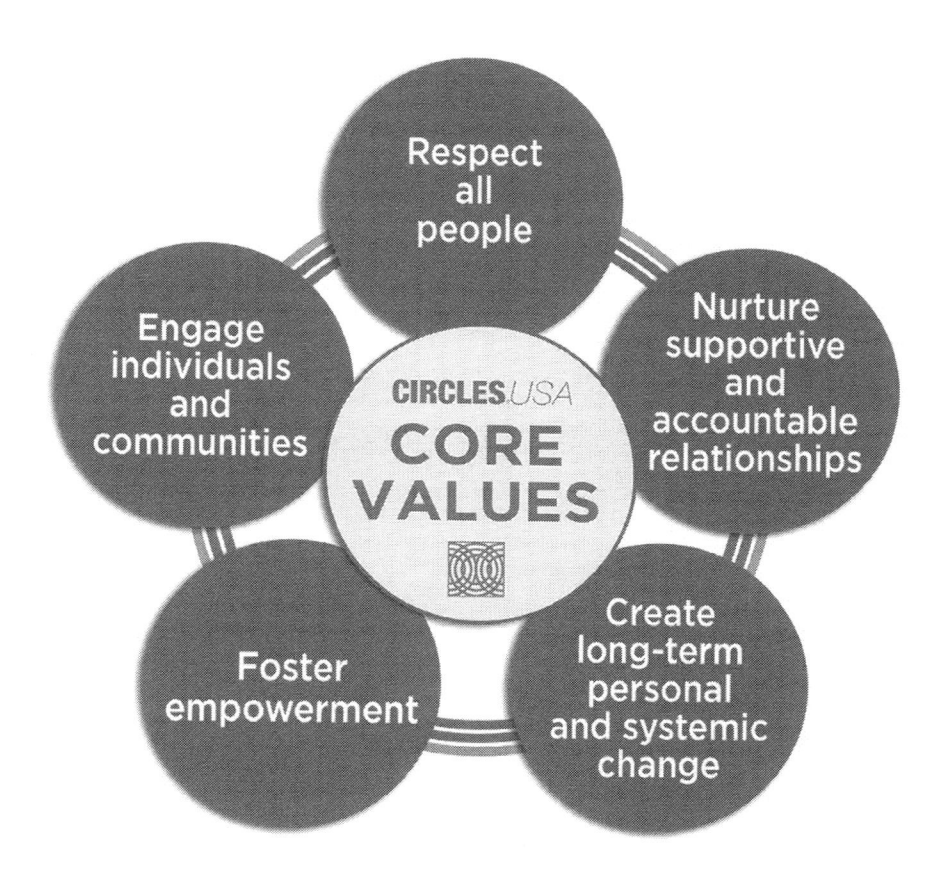

CIRCLES USA CORE VALUES
- Respect all people
- Nurture supportive and accountable relationships
- Create long-term personal and systemic change
- Foster empowerment
- Engage individuals and communities

The Circles USA board of directors uses these values to guide their strategic conversation in achieving our mission. I use these values when reviewing annual goals with our executive team. All training programs and materials are evaluated against these values. Going back to principle on a regular basis to guide decisions and to align actions leads to embedding the vision in the culture.

The change is truly embedded when you can walk away from the process and see the change continue through others. You have completed your transformational journey.

Self-Reflection Questions

- What structures must be in place to embed the transformation?

- What new leadership must be developed in order to sustain the changes?

- How am I personally feeling about the process? Do I feel completion? If not, what else must be completed?

- As this cycle of transformation ends, is there a new vision calling to me now? What is that?

Supporting the Next Generation of Leaders

Success is all about developing leaders.

Quick facts:
- Every day, 10,000 baby boomers retire.
- By 2020, 48% of the workforce will be millennials.
- 91% of millennials plan to stay at their current job fewer than three years.
- 67% of millennials are looking for a new job.
- In the next five years, 84% of organizations anticipate a shortage of leaders.
- 83% of organizations say it is important to develop leaders at all levels. *

All statistics are from Brandon Hall's State of Leadership Development 2015: Time to Act is Now.

Self-Reflection Questions

- Who are your next generation of leaders?

- What can you do now to identify and support them in being able to continue the transformational process beyond your leadership?

Be the Change: Center of the Map

> *Be the change you want to see happen instead of trying to change anyone else.* — Arleen Lorrance

At the center of the Transformational Map is you as the leader.

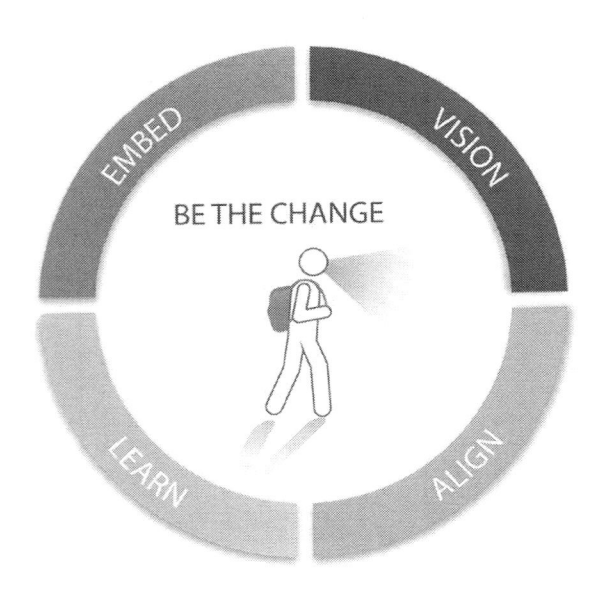

What must happen for your community must also be modeled in your own life. Look at how you want others to change, and then commit to making these changes in your own life. If you want people to become more empowered and permanently move out of poverty, take a look at some area of your life where you feel helpless—like a victim of circumstances beyond your control. Use the tools you want others to have on your own goals and move out of the victim space. Give yourself your own circle of Allies to help you make the shift. Remember this image and celebrate the feelings of change:

Completing our Transformational Journey

As your vision becomes embedded in the community and other people take up the mantle to continue its good works, your vision might open to something new. Don't be afraid to delegate, shift your position, and release your former vision to the next generation. It's time to celebrate and let go. You have changed and grown throughout your first cycle of the Transformational Map, so your vision might have shifted as well. It's time to turn your attention to what might be calling to you now.

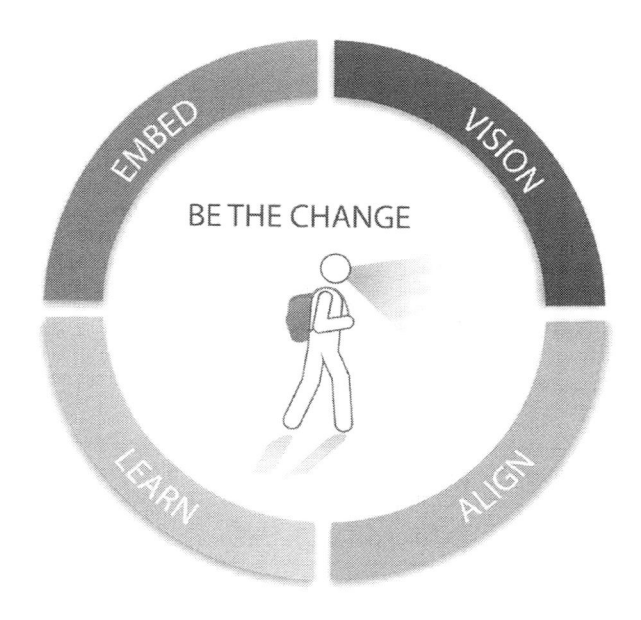

Made in the
USA
Lexington, KY